# breakfast & brunch

# breakfast & brunch

**delicious recipes to start the day**

**Tonia George**

photography by Jonathan Gregson

RYLAND
PETERS
& SMALL

LONDON NEW YORK

**Senior designer** Megan Smith
**Senior editor** Céline Hughes
**Production controller** Ros Holmes
**Art director** Leslie Harrington
**Publishing director** Alison Starling

**Food stylist** Tonia George
**Prop stylist** Liz Belton
**Assistant food stylist** Siobhan Boyle
**Indexer** Hilary Bird

First published in 2009 by
Ryland Peters & Small, Inc.
519 Broadway, 5th Floor
New York, NY 10012
www.rylandpeters.com

10 9 8 7 6 5 4 3 2 1

Text © Tonia George 2009
Design and photographs
© Ryland Peters & Small 2009

ISBN: 978-1-84597-910-2

Library of Congress Cataloging-in-
Publication Data

George, Tonia.
  Breakfast & brunch : delicious recipes to
start the day / Tonia George ; photography
by Jonathan Gregson.
    p. cm.
  ISBN 978-1-84597-910-2
  1. Breakfasts. 2. Brunches. I. Title.
  TX733.G46 2009
  641.5'2--dc22

                            2009016163

Printed and bound in China

## Notes

• All spoon measurements are level,
unless otherwise specified.
• Ovens should be preheated to the
specified temperature. Recipes in this book
were tested using a regular oven. If using a
convection oven, follow the manufacturer's
instructions for adjusting temperatures.
• All eggs are medium, unless otherwise
specified. Recipes containing raw or partially
cooked egg, or raw fish or shellfish, should
not be served to the very young, very old,
anyone with a compromised immune
system, or pregnant women.
• Sterilize preserving jars before use.
Wash them in hot, soapy water and rinse in
boiling water. Place in a large saucepan, then
cover with hot water. With the lid on, bring
the water to a boil and continue boiling for
15 minutes. Turn off the heat, then leave the
jars in the hot water until just before they
are to be filled. Invert the jars onto clean
paper towels to dry. Sterilize the lids for
5 minutes, by boiling, or according to the
manufacturer's instructions. Jars should be
filled and sealed while they are still hot.

# Contents

# Rise & shine!

Breakfast is by far and away my favorite meal of the day, which is ironic because mornings are probably my least favorite time of the day. Some days the thought of a frothy mocha and a slab of sourdough toast slathered in peanut butter is the only incentive there is to throw back the covers and face the world.

And if it's difficult enough to force yourself out of bed, it's an even tougher job luring other grumpy heads out of their warm, cozy slumber. That must be why typical breakfast and brunch dishes are so full of vibrant flavors; salty bacon, sweet ambrosial maple syrup, creamy eggs, steaming coffee, voluptuous yogurt, and zingy fruits. I defy anyone to sleep on contentedly once the smoky aromas of bacon frying and toast turning golden creep up their nostrils.

**Some days the thought of a frothy mocha and a slab of toast slathered in peanut butter is the only incentive there is to throw back the covers and face the world.**

Rushing out of the house with an empty tummy is never a good idea. Miss breakfast and research shows that you're more likely to suffer poor concentration and a slump in energy levels. Eating also kickstarts your metabolism and stabilizes blood sugar levels, so skipping a meal in the hope of saving on a few calories is counterproductive. Armed with the many recipes in this book, there really is no excuse. There are lots of quick ideas for rushed weekday mornings when everything seems to conspire against letting you leave the house on time, from Nutty Honey Granola (page 33) and Rhubarb & Orange Compote (page 29), to a five-minute Banana, Honey, & Wheat Germ Lassi (page 18) which can be wolfed down in a flash. Some you'll need to prepare on the weekend, but they promise to see you right through the week.

I have always been a huge fan of breakfast. When I was younger my mom made me toast before school every single morning—always one with Marmite and one with marmalade. If we were late for school the toast would be shimmied onto a paper towel and I'd finish it in the car. But when the weekend came around it was a different story. The whole family wandered about in their robes in a well-rehearsed formation, each with their own job: the chief toast maker, someone to make the coffee, and another at the stove turning slices of bacon and sausage links until the table was groaning with food.

On birthdays and Mother's Day the mornings would stretch a little further, sometimes into the afternoon. After appetites had been whetted with a Mimosa, we would dig into bowls of Greek yogurt scattered with pecans, drizzled with honey, and topped with chunks of tropical fruit. After a short break we'd be back for Blueberry Pancakes (page 89), light and fluffy enough to absorb twice their weight of maple syrup, or sometimes a buttery Smoked Haddock Kedgeree (page 113) hiding lovely chunks of fresh fish and still-soft boiled egg.

It's very insightful to see how people start their days. There are those that go for the sugar and caffeine rush of a coffee and a pastry, others who need a plateful of eggs and

Breakfast stirs up cozy, nostalgic memories evoking hearth and home, and having someone cook it for you makes you feel nurtured.

sausages alongside mountains of toast, and plenty of others still that dare not deviate from their more virtuous bowl of oats. I've included recipes to please all of you, from hurried weekday breakfasts to leisurely weekend brunches. In fact a weekend brunch is a good chance to try some of the more eclectic dishes. After the repetitive rhythm of the week, it's a time when I like to explore what other cultures eat. In England we've been doing this since the Victorian times, when kedgeree was introduced to the breakfast table from India. Likewise, in California, Huevos Rancheros (page 49) has now become a staple brunch fixture. There are many other dishes that I have borrowed for this book, such as Spain's delicious cinnamon sugar-coated Churros (page 78), and the Scandinavian Gravadlax (page 119), to modern Australian classics such as Corn Cakes with Bacon & Avocado (page 106) born of a love for fresh ingredients.

Of course, I'm very particular about what goes on my breakfast plate, and I find that most people are. Eggs must be cooked to perfection—for me this means they need to ooze with an ocherous yolk but for others any trace of wobble will have been left far behind. My bacon needs to be so crisp that it snaps, but you might find it too dry like this. And whereas some balk at the marriage of sweet maple syrup with smoky bacon, I couldn't imagine life without it. So feel free to adapt the recipes to suit your own set of foibles; that's exactly what makes us who we are.

More than any other meal, I've also noticed how breakfast turns grown adults back into fussy children. Look at the way people cling to their favorite childhood cereal all through their adult life, and never lose the wide-eyed pleasure at seeing a stack of pancakes dripping with butter. Breakfast stirs up cozy, nostalgic memories evoking hearth and home, and

having someone cook it for you makes you feel nurtured. This is what makes it a special meal.

I also find brunching to be a rather intimate ritual. Sharing your morning meal tends to be reserved for partners and family and so brunch is where friendships are cemented and intimate secrets spilled. You might breakfast alone, but it's never okay to brunch alone. Perhaps this is the only real difference in breakfasting and brunching, because after all, when exactly does a breakfast become a brunch? Does it depend on what, when or how much you eat? Is anything more than three slices of toast after noon considered brunch? There is no definitive answer. The actual term was recorded by Brit Guy Beringer in his visionary article "Brunch: A plea" published in *Hunter's Weekly* in 1895. He makes a case for replacing the post-hunt meal with a multi-course feast starting with more breakfast-friendly fare. "Brunch is cheerful,

sociable and compelling… and sweeps away the worries and cobwebs of the week," he wrote. It caught on in affluent social circles, but wasn't fully embraced until it crossed the Atlantic in the 1930s, where it took off as an indulgent Mother's Day treat.

Even now "doing brunch" implies a certain amount of hedonism. Stretching the morning meal into the afternoon hours usually comes about after an eventful evening which has encroached upon your night of sleep. This is what feels so decadent about brunch. It defies convention and is full of contradictions: you can ignore alarm clocks, eat something sweet before your savory course, enjoy cake before noon, and have a cocktail alongside a boiled egg. It is truly a time when you can do what you want to rather than what you should do —a sentiment that very much appeals as I roll over, smile contentedly, and switch off my bleeping alarm clock on a Saturday morning.

# drinks

Carrot, apple, & ginger juice  Pear, kiwi, & apple juice  **Basil limeade**
Pineapple & mint agua fresca  Pomegranate & orange sunrise  **Banana,
honey, & wheat germ lassi**  Cashew & mango smoothie  Raspberry,
strawberry, & orange juice  **Bloody mary**  Sea breeze  Blood orange &
campari mimosa  **Lemon & sage tisane**  Real hot chocolate  Spiced mocha

# Carrot, apple, & ginger juice

4 carrots
2 apples, quartered
1½ in. fresh ginger
ice, to serve
*a juicer*
**SERVES 2**

There is something about this blend of fruit and vegetables that feels so extremely virtuous and cleansing. It is very thirst-quenching as well, especially when served really well chilled. Great for a hangover.

Pass the carrots, apples, and ginger through a juicer, one at a time, into a pitcher. Add ice for 2 people and serve.

# Pear, kiwi, & apple juice

3 pears, quartered
3 kiwi fruit, quartered
1 apple, quartered
ice, to serve
*a juicer*
**SERVES 2**

Kiwis are my secret weapon against colds, being rich in vitamin C. They are sharp and sweet, and mixed with the mellower flavors of pears and apples they make a really gorgeous early-morning juice.

Pass the pears, kiwis, and apples through a juicer, one at a time, into a pitcher. Add ice for 2 people and serve.

# Basil limeade

1 scant cup freshly
   squeezed lime juice
   (from about 10 limes)
⅓ cup packed light brown
   sugar
a handful of fresh basil
   leaves
2 handfuls of ice
1 cup soda water
*4–6 cocktail glasses, chilled
   in the freezer for 1 hour*
**SERVES 4–6**

If I'm having a brunch gathering then this basil limeade is what I serve to guests. The amount of lime and sugar is a personal thing, so I suggest you adjust it to taste, adding more of one or the other as necessary. There will be guests who will appreciate a cheeky dash of cachaça rum in theirs for a caipirinha-style cocktail.

Put the lime juice, sugar, and basil in a blender (one that is able to crush ice) and blend until smooth. Add the ice and blend briefly to break up the ice cubes. Pour into the cocktail glasses and top up with the soda water.

*Basil limeade (right)*

## Pineapple & mint agua fresca

½ cup granulated sugar

a smallish pineapple (about
1¾ lbs.), peeled and
cored

a small handful of fresh
mint leaves, plus extra
to serve

ice, to serve

2⅓ cups chilled soda
water (optional)

**SERVES 4–8**

Refreshing *agua fresca* is found all over Mexico. The name literally means "cold water" and it can be any fruit (or even another ingredient such as tamarind or rice and milk) blended with ice, sugar, and water. The idea is that it is cooling and rehydrating on a hot day. Serve it as a whipped fruit frappé just with ice, or as a sparkling drink mixed with soda water.

Put the sugar and ½ cup water in a saucepan and heat gently until the sugar has dissolved. Remove from the heat and let cool while you cut the pineapple into rough chunks. Put the pineapple in a blender with the mint and the cooled syrup. Blend until smooth. Divide between 4 tumblers with a scoop of ice in each one, or 8 tall glasses and top up with ice and the soda water.

## Pomegranate & orange sunrise

ice, to serve

2 cups freshly squeezed
orange juice

¾ cup pure pomegranate
juice

**SERVES 2**

A twist on the usual tequila sunrise, mine is made with the newly fashionable pomegranate juice which adds a twist of bitterness to cut through the natural sweetness of orange juice. I sometimes add a shot of Campari to the pomegranate juice too, but this makes it an entirely different kind of morning!

Half fill 2 tumblers with ice and top up with orange juice so they are two-thirds full. Pour the pomegranate juice slowly down the side of the glass so it sinks to the bottom. Serve straightaway with a cocktail stirrer.

# Banana, honey, & wheat germ lassi

2 bananas, peeled
2 teaspoons honey
½ cup plain yogurt
⅔ cup whole milk
1 tablespoon wheat germ
or wheat bran
**SERVES 2**

Some mornings I need a smoothie which is a meal in itself, especially if I am awake early and can't face eating. With the added bite of the wheat germ, this lassi fits the bill. Lassi is a cooling Indian drink which can be sweet or savory. In the summer I add some ice before blending it for a more chilled drink. If you like ripe bananas, let the skins become speckled for a more intense experience.

Put the bananas, honey, yogurt, and milk in a blender and blend until smooth. Taste and add a little more honey if you think it needs it. Stir in the wheat germ and blend briefly just to mix. Divide between 2 tall glasses and serve with straws big enough for the wheat germ not to cause blockages.

# Cashew & mango smoothie

⅓ cup shelled cashews,
soaked overnight in cold
water
1 ripe mango, peeled and
pitted
1 teaspoon flaxseed
**SERVES 2**

It's easy to forget how milky blended cashews are, but they do make brilliant dairy-free smoothies. I like to blend mine with mango as it results in a super-thick smoothie verging on dessert territory. You could also use soft berries or bananas.

Drain the cashews and put in a blender with ⅔ cup water. Blend until you have a smooth, nutty milk. Roughly chop the mango and add to the blender. Blend again, then stir in the flaxseed. Divide between 2 tumblers and serve.

# Raspberry, strawberry, & orange juice

1 cup frozen raspberries
1 cup strawberries, hulled
1⅔ cups freshly squeezed
orange juice
**SERVES 2–4**

I like to keep raspberries in my freezer for a rainy day as they add body to smoothies as well as a sharp burst of fruity flavor. There's no need to add ice, as the raspberries will make the drink lovely and icy for you.

Put the raspberries, strawberries, and orange juice in a blender and blend until smooth. Divide between 2–4 tumblers and serve.

*Raspberry, strawberry, & orange juice; Banana, honey, & wheat germ lassi; and Cashew & mango smoothie (left to right)*

# Bloody mary

⅔ cup vodka

1 cup pure tomato juice

½ teaspoon hot
 horseradish sauce

1 teaspoon Worcestershire
 sauce

4 dashes Tabasco sauce

¼ teaspoon celery salt

½ teaspoon cracked black
 pepper

2 limes, cut into small
 wedges

ice, to serve

**SERVES 4**

There's nothing like a good Bloody Mary after a late night: it seems to get the blood pumping and cure any feelings of drowsiness. If you want a Virgin Mary leave out the vodka but squeeze in some more lime so you get more of a tang in it.

Mix all the ingredients together in a pitcher. Taste and adjust the seasonings if necessary, adding more heat, pepper, or lime as you wish. Add a couple of handfuls of ice and serve with a stack of tumblers.

## Sea breeze

a handful of ice

²⁄₃ cup pure pink grapefruit
   juice

1 ¹⁄₃ cups pure cranberry
   juice

¹⁄₂ cup vodka

1 lime, cut into wedges

*a cocktail shaker*

**SERVES 4**

**This is a great morning drink for summer. Simple to make and really refreshing but a few glasses will make you feel pleasantly sleepy, so watch you don't end up crawling back into bed.**

Put the ice in the cocktail shaker along with the juices and vodka. Squeeze over a couple of lime wedges. Put the top on the shaker and shake a few times. Strain into 2 tall glasses and add a lime wedge to each before serving.

## Blood orange & campari mimosa

2 cups pure blood orange
   juice

2 tablespoons Campari

750-ml bottle sparkling
   white wine, chilled

**SERVES 4**

**Mimosa is a standard offering at brunch gatherings, but this one is different. The Campari and blood orange make it a little bitter, and this really whets the appetite. If anyone needs his or hers sweetened—not everyone gets the bitter thing—add a dash of agave syrup or honey and serve with a cocktail stirrer.**

Divide the blood orange juice between 4 champagne flutes. Add a dash of Campari to each one, then top up with the wine.

*Blood orange & campari mimosa (above)*

# Lemon & sage tisane

a small handful of fresh
   sage leaves
1 lemon
2½ cups boiling water
1–2 teaspoons honey,
   to taste
**SERVES 2**

A tisane is a herbal tea, made strictly without real tea. Instead it is made by infusing herbs, spices, or any aromatics in hot water. My lemony tisane infused with sage is a great drink for the morning—it will brighten your eyes and leave your face with a warm glow, if nothing else.

Put the sage leaves in a teapot. Using a potato peeler, pare off the lemon zest leaving behind the white pith underneath. Add this to the teapot. Halve the slightly naked-looking lemon and squeeze out all its juice, then set aside. Pour the boiling water over the leaves and zest and let steep for 3–5 minutes, depending on how strong you like it. Pour into 2 mugs and add lemon juice and honey to taste.

# Real hot chocolate

2 cups whole milk
1 vanilla bean, split
   lengthwise
3½ oz. bittersweet
   chocolate (at least 70%
   cocoa solids), coarsely
   grated, plus extra to dust
1 tablespoon light brown
   sugar
**SERVES 2**

Once you have had proper hot chocolate there is no going back I'm afraid. Pick a really good cooking chocolate with at least 70% cocoa solids to make this, so that you get a really chocolatey flavor.

Pour the milk into a saucepan and add the vanilla bean. Slowly bring to a gentle simmer, then remove from the heat and set aside for 10 minutes to allow the flavor to infuse the milk. Add the chocolate and sugar and whisk into the milk until melted and dissolved. Return to a low heat until steaming, but not boiling. Remove the vanilla bean, then divide between 2 mugs. Dust with chocolate.

# Spiced mocha

1¼ cups whole milk
1 cinnamon stick
a pinch of grated nutmeg
2 shots of espresso coffee
2 tablespoons unsweetened
   cocoa powder
1–2 tablespoons demerara
   sugar
½ cup whipping cream,
   whipped to soft peaks
**SERVES 2**

I find coffee to be quite bitter but I love hot chocolate, so for me, this is the best of both worlds: the hit of caffeine with the luxurious sweetness of a good steaming mug of cocoa. The spices give it a real complexity and stop it becoming sickly sweet. I can't justify the whipped cream on top, but I think it would be foolish to make it without.

Pour the milk into a saucepan and add the cinnamon and nutmeg. Slowly bring to a gentle simmer, then remove from the heat and set aside for 10 minutes to allow the flavors to infuse the milk. Meanwhile, pour the espresso shots into a small heatproof pitcher. Stir in the cocoa powder and sugar until blended. Add the hot milk and whisk until all the ingredients are well blended. Return to the pan and reheat gently. Divide between 2 mugs and top with whipped cream.

# fruits & grains

Strawberries with pine nuts & greek yogurt  Melon salad in stem ginger syrup  **Poached pears in jasmine tea syrup with cinnamon & dates** Rhubarb & orange compote  Broiled pink grapefruit with vanilla sugar **Bircher muesli**  Toasted coconut & tropical fruit muesli  Nutty honey granola  **Porridge with apples & blackberries**  Deep coconut & sour cherry oat bars  Apricot & pumpkin seed granola bars  **Irish oatmeal with bananas, maple syrup, & pecans**  Granola, nectarine, & ricotta parfait

# Strawberries with pine nuts & greek yogurt

3 cups strawberries,
hulled and halved

2 tablespoons natural
cane sugar

3 tablespoons dark brown
sugar

1 cup Greek yogurt

3 tablespoons pine nuts

**SERVES 4**

When strawberries are at their most fragrant, with their cotton candy perfume, this is the perfect breakfast dish to whip up. Crumbling dark brown sugar over the voluptuous Greek yogurt creates a pool of fudginess on top. All the treacly flavors which come from the natural molasses in the sugar are drawn out; these contrast beautifully against the yogurt and enhance the sweet berries.

Put the strawberries in a bowl and scatter over the natural cane sugar. Cover and set aside for 10 minutes. Scatter the dark brown sugar over the yogurt in a separate bowl and set aside. Meanwhile, put the pine nuts in a heavy-based skillet over low heat and toast for 2–3 minutes, shaking them about until they become golden on all sides.

Divide the strawberries between 4 bowls. Swirl the now fudgy brown sugar through the yogurt and spoon on top of the strawberries. Scatter the pine nuts on top of the strawberries and serve.

# Melon salad in stem ginger syrup

½ cup packed light brown
sugar

2 oz. stem ginger, drained
and finely chopped

freshly squeezed juice of
1 lemon

1 cantaloupe melon, peeled
and seeded

1¼ cups raspberries
(optional)

**SERVES 4**

Ginger and melon are quite simply a match made in culinary heaven. The sweetness of one sets off the sharpness of the other one and vice versa. Make this when melons are bursting with ripe perfume and the raspberries, if you'd like to use some, are as sweet as can be.

Put the light brown sugar in a saucepan with the ginger and ¾ cup water. Heat gently until the sugar has completely dissolved, then turn up the heat and simmer for 5 minutes. Remove from the heat and add the lemon juice. Let cool.

Slice or chop the melon, place in a bowl, and pour over the syrup. Tumble over the raspberries, if using, then serve.

# Poached pears in jasmine tea syrup with cinnamon & dates

¾ cup boiling water

1 tablespoon jasmine tea leaves

2 cinnamon sticks

⅓ cup honey

4 small pears, peeled, halved, and cored

1½ cups Medjool dates, pitted and sliced

plain yogurt or ricotta, to serve

**SERVES 4**

I love using tea leaves to imbue syrups with a delicate flavor. Jasmine tea is one of the most fragrant flavors, especially if you look out for the high-quality teas whose leaves are furled into long shapes.

Allow the boiling water to cool for a few minutes so it doesn't scorch the delicate tea leaves. Once it has cooled slightly—ideally 195°F, but don't worry, you don't need to check with a thermometer—you can pour it onto the jasmine tea leaves in a teapot or a heatproof pitcher. Let it steep for 3 minutes.

Strain the jasmine tea into a saucepan. Add the cinnamon and honey and place over medium heat. Bring it to a gentle simmer, then lower in the pears.

Cut out a disk of parchment paper to fit inside the pan, scrunch it up, then open it out again. Lower it into the pan and cover with the lid. Simmer gently for 8 minutes, then turn the pears so the other side sees the syrup (replacing the paper disk and lid). Simmer for 8 minutes. Add the dates and simmer for 5 minutes (still with the paper disk and lid on). Remove from the heat and let stand for 10 minutes. Serve warm or cold with plain yogurt or ricotta.

# Rhubarb & orange compote

14 oz. rhubarb (about
  6 stalks)

grated zest of ½ orange

freshly squeezed juice
  of 1 orange

1 vanilla bean, split
  lengthwise

¾ cup packed light brown
  sugar

plain yogurt or hot cereal,
  to serve

**SERVES 4**

Add blueberries or strawberries to this basic cushion of pink rhubarb. Keep your eye out for bright pink forced rhubarb, which is grown indoors in the dark for its lurid color, making it an uplifting winter treat.

Preheat the oven to 350°F.

Trim the rhubarb to remove any leaves and the tough ends and cut into 3-inch lengths. Put these stubby bits of rhubarb, along with the orange zest, juice, and vanilla bean in a large baking dish and scatter the sugar over the top. Cover the dish with aluminum foil and roast in the preheated oven for 15–20 minutes, until the rhubarb compliantly softens up.

Let cool and serve with a generous dollop of yogurt or a bowl of steaming hot cereal, or simply by itself. Store in the fridge for up to 1 week.

# Broiled pink grapefruit with vanilla sugar

2 pink grapefruits
1 vanilla bean, split
   lengthwise
2 tablespoons sugar
plain yogurt, to serve
   (optional)

**SERVES 4**

This is a quick and easy way to serve zingy grapefruit. If you happen to have one of those snazzy curved grapefruit knives, now is the moment you have been waiting for. You really do need to loosen the flesh from the rind before you broil it, as a hot grapefruit becomes quite dangerous when you try to delve into it with a spoon. Don't fret if you don't have a grapefruit knife—a small paring knife does a good job too.

Halve the grapefruit and slice a little off each top and bottom so they sit securely on a flat surface. Loosen the flesh from the rind with a curved grapefruit knife or small paring knife.

Scrape the seeds out of the vanilla bean and add to the sugar. Mix thoroughly with the back of a spoon to spread out the seeds.

Preheat the broiler.

Place each grapefruit half on the broiler pan and sprinkle the sugar over them. Slide under the broiler and let the sugar melt and caramelize. It should only take 2–3 minutes. Remove from under the broiler and let cool for 2 minutes. Serve with plain yogurt on the side or if you are being abstemious, by itself.

# Bircher muesli

1 cup rolled oats
½ cup golden raisins
¾ cup apple juice
freshly squeezed juice of
   1 lemon
¼ cup plain yogurt
1 apple, cored, peeled,
   and grated
3 tablespoons flaked
   almonds
mixed summer berries,
   to serve
honey, to serve

**SERVES 4–6**

This is what I like to call summer porridge. It has the type of texture you either love or hate. I adore it—there is something comforting about its soggy sweetness —but my husband prefers crunchy granola. Each to his own. It will keep for 2–3 days in the fridge, but in that case, leave the apple out so it doesn't brown.

Put the oats and raisins in a large dish. Pour over the apple and lemon juices. Cover with a kitchen towel and let soak overnight. Alternatively place everything in an airtight container and stick in the fridge, especially if it is very hot.

The next morning when you're ready for breakfast, stir the yogurt, apple, and almonds into the soaked muesli. Divide between 4–6 bowls, scatter some brightly colored berries over the top, and finish with a zigzag of honey.

*Bircher muesli (right)*

# Toasted coconut & tropical fruit muesli

2⅓ cups rolled oats

⅓ cup black (or white) sesame seeds

⅓ cup sunflower seeds

½ cup apple juice

3 tablespoons vegetable oil

⅓ cup desiccated coconut

⅓ cup finely chopped dried mango

⅓ cup finely chopped dried pineapple

⅓ cup finely chopped dried papaya

*1 large baking sheet, lined with parchment paper*

**SERVES 6–8**

This toasted muesli is made with apple juice instead of being coated in sugar or honey, as most granola is. It crisps up the oats, but isn't overly sweet. I like the chewy tanginess of tropical fruits, but any dried fruits will work as they are simply stirred in at the end. If you can find some black sesame seeds, often sold in Asian grocers, they stand out more, but the regular ones are fine too.

Preheat the oven to 300°F.

Pour the oats and seeds into a really large mixing bowl, then stir in the apple juice and oil. Toss well until the juice has soaked into the dry ingredients. Tip half of the mixture onto the prepared baking sheet and spread out evenly. Bake in the preheated oven for 25 minutes, until the oats are starting to toast.

Remove the baking sheet from the oven and give everything a good stir. Add the desiccated coconut to the oat mixture and bake for a further 20 minutes. Let cool completely.

When the muesli is cold, stir in all the chopped dried fruit and toss to distribute evenly. Store in an airtight container and eat within 3 weeks.

# Nutty honey granola

½ cup pure maple syrup

½ cup honey

¼ cup sunflower oil

2 cups rolled oats

⅔ cup shelled almonds, roughly chopped

⅔ cup shelled Brazil nuts, roughly chopped

⅓ cup shelled pumpkin seeds

½ teaspoon salt

⅔ cup golden raisins

*1 large baking sheet, lined with parchment paper*

**SERVES 10–12**

Mmmm, crunchy honeyed granola. This version is very sweet and crunchy and quite rich so you don't need a lot. I tend to have a scattering with my yogurt rather than the other way round. The trick is to get it to brown evenly, so you need it to be spread out and to turn it during roasting. Don't let it become too dark or it gets bitter. If in doubt, take it out and let it cool a little, then taste it and you can always put it back in for longer.

Preheat the oven to 275°F.

Put the maple syrup, honey, and oil in a small saucepan and set over low heat to warm though. Put the oats, nuts, seeds, and salt in a large mixing bowl and stir well. Pour over the warmed syrup and mix thoroughly with a wooden spoon. All the oats must be moistened.

Spread the granola over the prepared baking sheet, making sure it is no deeper than ½ inch, and bake in the preheated oven for 20 minutes.

Remove the sheet from the oven and stir the toasted, golden granola from the edges to the center, then smooth out again. Return to the oven for a further 15–20 minutes, until lightly golden. Don't expect it to become crunchy—the mixture will remain soft until it cools.

Remove from the oven and let cool for 10 minutes before stirring in the raisins. Let cool completely, then break into pieces. Store in an airtight container and eat within 1 month.

*Nutty honey granola (left)*

## Porridge with apples & blackberries

**¾ cup rolled oats**

**1 cup whole milk,**
**plus a little extra to thin**

**a pinch of salt**

**½ cup raisins**

**1 tablespoon butter**

**2 apples, cored and cut**
**into slim wedges**

**3 tablespoons demerara**
**sugar**

**a pinch of ground**
**cinnamon**

**1 cup blackberries**

**SERVES 4**

Everyone likes their porridge prepared differently. Personally I find porridge made with all milk too cloying and when it's made with just water a little insipid, unless you add a swirl of cream at the end which rather defeats the purpose of using good old water. A pinch of salt is a must too, as this stops it from being flabby and gives it some backbone.

Put the oats in a saucepan and add the milk and 1 cup water. Add a pinch of salt, cover with a lid, and slowly bring to a boil over medium heat. Once the mixture is bubbling, turn the heat to low, add the raisins, and cook for 2–3 minutes, stirring occasionally. The porridge should be thick and creamy. Take off the heat and let stand with a lid on for 2–3 minutes while you cook the apples.

Put the butter in a skillet over high heat until the bubbling subsides. Stir in the apples, sugar, and cinnamon. Let caramelize for 2–3 minutes, then flip the apple wedges over so the other side gets a chance to become golden too. Finally, add the blackberries and heat for a couple of minutes just so they warm through a little.

Meanwhile, spoon the porridge into 4 bowls and stir in a little cold milk to stop it becoming too thick. Spoon the caramelized apples and blackberries on top and serve straightaway.

# Deep coconut & sour cherry oat bars

2/3 cup dried sour cherries

6½ tablespoons unsalted butter, cubed

½ cup light corn syrup

¾ cup light brown sugar

½ teaspoon ground cinnamon

½ cup desiccated coconut

1¾ cups rolled oats

½ cup plus 1 tablespoon self-rising flour

½ teaspoon baking soda

a pinch of salt

an 8 x 8-in. baking pan, lined with parchment paper

**MAKES 9**

These oat bars flecked with dried cherries are chewy and moist. The butter and syrupy sweetness in them are usually reserved for an indulgent teatime treat, but they also go down very well in the morning.

Preheat the oven to 350°F.

Put the cherries in a bowl of boiling water and let soak for 10 minutes.

Meanwhile, put the butter, corn syrup, and sugar in a saucepan and heat gently until dissolved and melted. Stir in the cinnamon. Pour the coconut, oats, flour, baking soda, and salt over the butter mixture and stir to combine. Drain the cherries and add those. Once everything is well mixed, pack the mixture into the prepared baking pan, pressing it down with the back of a spoon to compact it. Bake in the preheated oven for 25–30 minutes, until golden at the sides.

Remove from the oven and let cool for 10 minutes. Turn the mixture out onto a cutting board and cut into 9 squares. Let cool, then store in an airtight container and eat within 5 days.

# Apricot & pumpkin seed granola bars

1¾ cups rolled oats

2/3 cup shelled pumpkin seeds

1/3 cup wheat germ or wheat bran

½ teaspoon ground ginger

½ teaspoon salt

2/3 cup dried apricots, chopped

2/3 cup honey

¼ cup packed light brown sugar

1/3 cup sunflower oil

an 8 x 12-in. baking pan, lined with parchment paper

**MAKES 14**

In the name of good health, I have come up with a crunchier, snappier, less buttery bar than those above. They are not chewy but they will hit the spot in the morning. You can vary the dried fruit and spice as much as you like as long as you stick to the basic premise.

Preheat the oven to 350°F.

Put the oats, pumpkin seeds, wheat germ, ginger, salt, and apricots in a large mixing bowl. Put the honey, sugar, and oil in a saucepan over low heat. Heat for 4–5 minutes, until the sugar has melted into the butter.

Remove from the heat and pour the melted mixture over the dry ingredients in the mixing bowl, stirring so the mixture moistens all over. Spoon the mixture into the prepared baking pan and smooth it out with the back of a spoon. Bake in the preheated oven for 20–22 minutes, until golden around the edges.

Remove from the oven and let cool for 10 minutes. Turn the mixture out onto a cutting board and cut into 14 bars. Let cool, then store in an airtight container and eat within 5 days.

*Apricot & pumpkin seed granola bars, and Deep coconut & sour cherry oat bars (left to right)*

# Irish oatmeal with bananas, maple syrup, & pecans

1¼ cups Irish or steel-cut
    oats
a pinch of salt
⅓ cup shelled pecans,
    chopped
3 tablespoons heavy cream
2 bananas, sliced
pure maple syrup, to serve
**SERVES 4–6**

For proper oatmeal you will need to buy oats that haven't been rolled. These are called Irish, steel-cut, or pinhead oats and are coarser than rolled oats. This means a lot of extra cooking, which in turn means you need to reorganize yourself and put the oats on before you feed your cats, shower etc., and then you won't have to wait for them. The result is a much more al dente mass of oaty nuggets in a creamy risotto-like sauce. They also need a generous pinch of salt.

Heat 5 cups water in a heavy-based saucepan until it comes to a boil, then tip in the oats and salt. Cover with a lid and turn the heat down as low as possible so there is no danger of sticking.

Put the pecans in a dry skillet over medium heat and leave them to heat up. Stir so they brown evenly, then remove from the heat and set aside.

Go off and have your shower or walk the dog and, after 30 minutes, the oats will be ready. Check they are not sticking after about 20 minutes, the first time you cook them. After that you will have it all sussed out.

Stir in the cream, then spoon into bowls and scatter over the bananas and pecans. Serve with maple syrup.

# Granola, nectarine, & ricotta parfait

⅔ cup plain yogurt,
    preferably sheep's milk
1 cup ricotta
2 cups Nutty Honey
    Granola (page 33)
4 nectarines, pitted
    and sliced
⅔ cup raspberries
¼ cup honey, plus extra
    to drizzle
**SERVES 4**

These little pots of deliciousness are perfect to offer guests at a brunch party as an alternative to the fat-laden fry-up. Layer the ricotta, fruit, and granola in glasses for a groovy look. You can vary the fruit depending on the season, but if you use hard fruits, such as apples or pears, poach them in some sugar syrup first until they are as soft as a ripe nectarine.

Put the yogurt and ricotta in a bowl and beat together until combined.

Divide half the granola between 4 glasses, then put some nectarine slices and raspberries on top of that. Top with some of the yogurt mixture and honey.

Top with the remaining granola, followed by more nectarines and raspberries, saving a few for the top, and another spoonful or two of the yogurt mixture. Arrange the remaining fruit on top, drizzle with more honey, and serve straightaway.

*Granola, nectarine, & ricotta parfait (right)*

# eggs

Eggs benedict  Fried eggs with sage pangritata, asparagus, & pancetta **Herb fritters with fried eggs & sumac tomatoes** Poached eggs on spinach with yogurt & spiced butter  Eggs en cocotte with leeks & tapenade  **Scrambled eggs with smoked trout & shiso**  Huevos rancheros Soft-boiled eggs with prosciutto-wrapped focaccia  **Caramelized belgian endive with black forest ham & poached eggs**  French toast with provolone & half-dried tomatoes  Omelet with chives & gruyère **Smoked haddock, radish, & avocado omelet wraps**  Tortilla with potatoes, chiles, & piquillo peppers  Wild mushroom mini-frittatas with garlic sourdough croutons

# Eggs benedict

4 extra-large eggs

4 whole-grain English muffins, halved horizontally

8 slices of thin-cut ham

freshly ground black pepper

**HOLLANDAISE SAUCE**

2 tablespoons white wine vinegar

1 shallot, roughly chopped

½ teaspoon black peppercorns

2 large egg yolks

1 stick unsalted butter

**SERVES 4**

**This dish is all about timing. Get everything ready before you cook the eggs and you won't have to rush. Hollandaise sauce made in a blender is easy—just add the butter very slowly and you should hear the sauce turning thick and slushy.**

Preheat the broiler.

To make the hollandaise sauce, put the vinegar, 2 tablespoons cold water, the shallot, and peppercorns in a saucepan and simmer over low heat for a few minutes until you have 1 tablespoon liquid remaining. Strain into a blender (or in a bowl if you are going to use an electric handheld whisk) with the egg yolks and set aside. Melt the butter in the same pan.

Fill a large, deep skillet with water and bring to a demure simmer. Crack the eggs around the edge so they don't touch and poach for exactly 3 minutes.

Put the muffins (cut side up) and ham on a broiler pan and broil for 2–3 minutes.

To finish the sauce, blend the eggs and vinegar until frothy. With the motor still running, add the melted butter in a very slow trickle until the sauce is thick. You should take about a minute to add all the butter. Any quicker and it will not emulsify and you'll be left with runny eggs.

Drape a slice of ham on top of each muffin half. Scoop out each poached egg and add to the stack. Pour over the hollandaise sauce and sprinkle with a grinding of black pepper.

# Fried eggs with sage pangritata, asparagus, & pancetta

2 slices of sourdough bread, torn into chunks, crust and all

5 tablespoons olive oil

10 fresh sage leaves, shredded

14 oz. asparagus, trimmed

3½ oz. pancetta, cubed

4 extra-large eggs

sea salt and freshly ground black pepper

**SERVES 4**

**Roasting asparagus is my favorite way of cooking it: the flavor is intensified and the ends get frazzled. Pangritata—fried bread crumbs with herbs—was devised by the Italians to provide a similar texture and flavor to Parmesan, but cheaply.**

Preheat the oven to 375°F.

Whizz the bread in a food processor until you get chunky, uneven crumbs. Tip out onto a baking sheet and drizzle over 2 tablespoons of the oil, the sage, and some seasoning. Toss everything together, then bake in the preheated oven for 15 minutes, stirring a couple of times to ensure it browns evenly.

Snap off the pale, woody ends of the asparagus and discard. Put the stems on a baking sheet, drizzle with 2 tablespoons of the oil, and season. Toss, then scatter

the pancetta over the top. Roast in the oven for 10–12 minutes, until the pancetta is cooked through and the asparagus is tender and slightly frazzled.

Heat the remaining oil in a skillet over high heat, then crack an egg in each corner and turn the heat right down. Cook for 2–3 minutes until the white has set. If you need to firm up the white, cover with the lid for 30 seconds.

Divide the asparagus between 4 plates, top with an egg, and sprinkle the pangritata over the top.

*Eggs benedict (right)*

# Herb fritters with fried eggs & sumac tomatoes

4 or 5 plum tomatoes,
roughly chopped

2 teaspoons ground sumac

3 tablespoons extra virgin
olive oil, or more

5 extra-large eggs

1 teaspoon ground cumin

2 big handfuls of fresh
flatleaf parsley, leaves
roughly chopped and
stalks discarded

1 small handful of cilantro,
leaves roughly chopped
and stalks discarded

sea salt and freshly ground
black pepper

**SERVES 4**

**Sumac is a wild berry which, when dried and ground, adds a sour tang to food, a little like lemon juice. These herb fritters are a good way of using up leaves from a bush of herbs that needs trimming back. Serve it for a low-carb breakfast.**

Preheat the oven to low.

Put the tomatoes and sumac in a bowl with 1 tablespoon of the oil. Season and toss until coated, then set aside.

Crack one of the eggs into a mixing bowl, season, add the cumin, and beat to mix. Stir in the herbs. It will look like there is not enough egg, but you only need enough to bind it.

Heat a skillet over high heat and add 1 tablespoon of the oil. Drop 2 tablespoons of the herb mixture in the skillet to make your first fritter and continue until you run out of space in the skillet. Cook over high heat for 2 minutes on each side, until lightly golden. Keep warm in the oven while you fry the rest.

Once all the fritters are done, add the remaining oil to the same skillet and wait for it to heat up. Crack the remaining eggs into the skillet and fry for 2 minutes. Cover with a lid and cook for a further 30–40 seconds just to cook the top of the whites; you want the egg yolk to remain runny.

Divide the fritters between 4 plates, top with a fried egg, and scatter the sumac tomatoes over the top.

# Poached eggs on spinach with yogurt & spiced butter

1 small garlic clove, crushed

¾ cup Greek yogurt

3 tablespoons butter

½ teaspoon cumin seeds

½ teaspoon dried hot
pepper flakes

½ teaspoon sea salt flakes

1 loaf of Turkish flat bread,
cut into 4 squares and
halved horizontally

1 tablespoon olive oil

14 oz. spinach

8 extra-large eggs

sea salt and freshly ground
black pepper

**SERVES 4**

**This egg dish is popular in Australia where there is a big Turkish community. It is a great dish packed with so much flavor that you will be hooked from the first taste. If you can't get hold of Turkish bread then pita or sourdough work well.**

Preheat the broiler to high.

Get everything ready before you start cooking: mix the garlic and yogurt. Put the butter, cumin, pepper flakes, and salt flakes in a small saucepan. Put the flat bread on a baking sheet. Fill 2 deep skillets with water and bring to a boil over high heat.

Heat a wok, then add the oil and when hot, add the spinach in batches. Toss around the wok so it cooks evenly and when it is just wilted, take it off the heat, season, and cover.

Reduce the heat under the 2 skillets to low so the water is barely simmering and break 4 eggs, far apart, into each skillet. Leave for 3 minutes. Broil the bread, cut side up, until lightly toasted, then transfer to 4 plates. Spread some garlic yogurt over the bread and heap a mound of spinach on top. Using a slotted spoon, sit a poached egg on top of each square of yogurty bread. Quickly heat the spiced butter over high heat until bubbling, pour over the eggs, and serve.

*Poached eggs on spinach with yogurt & spiced butter (left)*

# Eggs en cocotte with leeks & tapenade

2 tablespoons butter

2 leeks, thinly sliced

a pinch of ground nutmeg

2 tablespoons tapenade
(olive paste)

4 extra-large eggs

2 tablespoons heavy cream

sea salt and freshly ground
black pepper

whole-grain toast or green
salad, to serve

*4 x 5-oz. ramekins*

**SERVES 4**

**Eggs *en cocotte*—baked eggs—are all about timing: you want that yolk to have a good molten ooze. Don't skip the *bain marie* part otherwise the whites will become overheated and tough. If you like you can put some chopped sautéed mushrooms or pesto in the base of the ramekins. Sometimes I buy porcini and truffle paste from a deli and use that, as it has such a natural affinity with eggs.**

Preheat the oven to 400°F.

Heat the butter in a skillet, add the leeks, and cook gently for 5–6 minutes until soft. Season to taste with salt, pepper, and nutmeg.

Spoon an equal amount of tapenade into each ramekin, then top with the leeks. Break an egg into each ramekin, season them too, then drizzle a trickle of the cream over the top of each.

Put the ramekins in a deep roasting pan in the oven and pour enough boiling water directly from the kettle into the roasting pan so that it comes about halfway up the sides of the ramekins. This is the *bain marie*. Bake in the preheated oven for 10–14 minutes—10 minutes if you like the yolks to remain runny, and a few minutes more if you prefer them set.

Lift the ramekins carefully out of the roasting pan using tongs or a kitchen towel and serve straightaway as they will continue to cook. Serve with whole-grain toast or a green salad on the side.

# Scrambled eggs with smoked trout & shiso

10 extra-large eggs

¼ cup whole milk

3 tablespoons butter

4 slices of white bread

9 oz. smoked trout, flaked

a handful of shiso cress
or radish sprouts

a pinch of Japanese hot
pepper or ground
red chile

sea salt and freshly ground
black pepper

**SERVES 4**

**Scrambled eggs need to be cooked with patience to become creamy. If they are cooked properly, you will not have to resort to adding cream, which just hides an underlying bad scramble. Smoked trout goes exceedingly well with scrambled eggs and the pretty purple leaves of shiso cress decorate it and add a spicy kick.**

Break the eggs into a mixing bowl and beat together with the milk and some salt and pepper.

Meanwhile, heat half the butter in a heavy-based saucepan over low heat until the bubbling subsides. Pour in the eggs and heat through, stirring occasionally, for 4–5 minutes, until they start to feel like they are in danger of sticking on the base of the pan. Reduce the heat to its lowest setting and stir constantly for 3–5 minutes to make sure the eggs are not overheating on the bottom of the pan.

Meanwhile, toast and butter the bread with the remaining butter. Take the eggs off the heat while they still look a little runny, add the trout, give them a final few stirs, and divide between the pieces of toast. Scatter the shiso and a little hot pepper over the top.

*Scrambled eggs with smoked trout & shiso (right)*

# Huevos rancheros

3 tablespoons vegetable oil

1 jalapeño or serrano chile, chopped

2 garlic cloves, crushed

1 lb. vine-ripened tomatoes, cut into slim wedges

14-oz. can pinto beans

1/2 cup grated sharp cheddar cheese

freshly squeezed juice of 1 lime, plus extra lime wedges to serve

a handful of cilantro leaves, chopped

4 eggs

4 corn tortillas

sea salt and freshly ground black pepper

**SERVES 4**

I like to cook my salsa with fresh tomatoes and then serve it with mashed, cheesy beans and these huevos rancheros. You can buy cans of refried beans but it is just as easy to mash your own. If you want to serve it with a spoonful of guacamole or sour cream, that's a great idea.

Heat 1 tablespoon of the oil in a large skillet over medium heat, then add the chile, half the garlic, and a pinch of salt and fry for 1–2 minutes, until softened. Add the tomatoes and cook gently for about 20 minutes.

Heat the remaining oil in a small saucepan, add the remaining garlic, and heat through for 20 seconds, until just browning. Add the beans, then using a potato masher, coarsely mash the beans and stir in plenty of salt and pepper and the cheese.

Stir the lime juice and cilantro into the tomato sauce. Make 4 holes in the sauce and crack an egg into each one. Cook for 3 minutes until set. Cover with the lid for the last 30 seconds just to firm up the whites.

Meanwhile, heat a skillet over medium heat. Cook the tortillas for 1 minute on each side, until golden and hot. Transfer to 4 plates and spread the beans over the tortillas. Top with tomato salsa and the eggs. Serve with lime wedges and guacamole or sour cream if you like.

# Soft-boiled eggs with prosciutto-wrapped focaccia

1 teaspoon anchovy paste

3 tablespoons extra virgin olive oil

8 x 1/2-in. slices of rosemary focaccia, halved horizontally

4 extra-large eggs, at room temperature

8 slices of prosciutto, each torn in half

**SERVES 4**

The method below is by far the best for soft-boiling eggs. In fact, the word "boiled" is misleading because boiling an egg toughens up the white, making it rubbery, not creamy. The timings here will give you a perfectly runny yolk with a set, creamy white. This will only work if the eggs are at room temperature to start with—don't cook them straight out of the fridge otherwise they will crack.

Preheat the broiler.

Mix the anchovy paste with the oil and spread it over the focaccia. Bring a medium saucepan of water to a rolling boil. Lower in the eggs and turn the heat down so they simmer gently for 1 minute. Turn off the heat completely, cover with a lid, and set your timer for 4 minutes.

Meanwhile, broil the focaccia, anchovy side up, for 1–2 minutes. Remove from the broiler and wrap a piece of prosciutto around each toast. Place on a plate with an egg cup. Remove the eggs from the water with a slotted spoon and transfer to the egg cups. Eat immediately otherwise the eggs will continue to cook.

*Huevos rancheros (left)*

# Caramelized belgian endive with black forest ham & poached eggs

2 tablespoons butter

4 heads Belgian endive, halved lengthwise

4 eggs

3½ oz. arugula

8 slices of Black Forest ham

1 oz. Parmesan, shaved

sea salt and freshly ground black pepper

**DRESSING**

1 small garlic clove, finely chopped

1 red chile, finely chopped

1 tablespoon red wine vinegar

2 tablespoons extra virgin olive oil

finely grated zest and juice of ½ unwaxed lemon

**SERVES 4**

Belgian endive is such an underrated vegetable, unlike in France and Italy where they use it a lot, and not just in the salad bowl. It is so different when cooked, becoming silky smooth and slightly bitter, which is why it works so well against a sweet, smoky ham like Black Forest ham. The chile and lemon in the dressing wake up all the flavors. If you make this once you'll be addicted.

Preheat the oven to low.

To make the dressing, put the garlic, chile, and vinegar in a bowl and whisk in the olive oil and lemon zest and juice.

Heat the butter in a large skillet over low heat and add the endive, cut side down. Season with salt and pepper, cover with a lid, and let the endive cook gently for 5–6 minutes. Remove the lid, turn up the heat, and continue to cook for 5 minutes, until the endive is golden. Turn the endive halves over and cook for 3–4 minutes so the other side gets a chance to caramelize. Transfer to the oven to keep warm.

Fill a large, deep skillet with water and bring to a demure simmer. Crack the eggs around the edge so they don't touch and poach for exactly 3 minutes.

Place a little mound of arugula on each plate, top with 2 endive halves and drape the Black Forest ham on top. Scoop out each poached egg and place on top of the ham. Scatter some Parmesan shavings around the plate and finish with a drizzle of dressing.

# French toast with provolone & half-dried tomatoes

4 eggs

⅔ cup whole milk

4 thick slices of challah

1 tablespoon pesto

3½ oz. provolone or mozzarella, thinly sliced

6 half-dried tomatoes, chopped

a handful of fresh basil leaves

2 tablespoons olive oil

sea salt and freshly ground black pepper

**SERVES 4**

French toast works really well as a savory dish, too. This one is not dissimilar to the Italian *mozzarella in carrozza*, where a mozzarella sandwich dipped in egg is fried. You can vary the filling, adding ham or salami if you like. The important thing is that you soak the bread so it absorbs all the egg and finish it off in the oven after frying as it won't cook all the way through like a thin French toast.

Preheat the oven to 350°F.

Put the eggs and milk in a bowl and whisk together with a little salt and pepper. Using a paring knife, make a pocket in each slice of challah by cutting horizontally into the center of one of the long sides. Spread a quarter of the pesto on the inside of each pocket, then fill with the provolone, tomatoes, and basil. Place in a shallow dish, pour in the egg mixture and set aside for 10 minutes.

Heat the oil in a skillet over high heat and fry the bread for 1–2 minutes on each side, until golden. Transfer to a baking sheet and bake in the preheated oven for 10 minutes, until puffed up.

*Caramelized belgian endive with black forest ham & poached eggs (right)*

# Omelet with chives & gruyère

3 eggs

2 tablespoons snipped
  fresh chives

1 tablespoon butter

2 tablespoons grated
  Gruyère cheese

1 tablespoon heavy cream

sea salt and freshly ground
  black pepper

*an 8-in. skillet*

**SERVES 1**

A perfectly crumpled, soft omelet oozing with cheese is bliss. Too many omelets are cooked badly, but once you master the technique, there's no end of combinations you can make. I love this indulgent filling, which complements, as opposed to overpowers the egg element of the omelet.

Gently beat the eggs in a bowl and season with salt and pepper. Stir in half the chives.

Heat the skillet over high heat until really hot. Add the butter, wait for it to sizzle, then just as it wants to brown pour in the eggs. Let them become nicely golden on the outside—no more than 45 seconds—drawing the cooked edges into the center. Tilt the skillet so the uncooked egg runs into the edges. When the omelet is evenly set, except for a little unset egg, it is done.

Remove the skillet from the heat and add the Gruyère and cream in the center. Fold 2 edges of the omelet over, then tilt the skillet so you can slide it out and upturn it onto a plate, seam side down. Grind some pepper over the top and finish with the remaining chives.

# Smoked haddock, radish, & avocado omelet wraps

6 eggs

about 2 tablespoons butter

6½ oz. hot smoked
  haddock, flaked

2 handfuls of watercress

1 ripe avocado, peeled,
  pitted, and chopped

6 radishes, thinly sliced

2 tablespoons extra virgin
  olive oil

2 tablespoons freshly
  squeezed lemon juice

sea salt and freshly ground
  black pepper

*a 6–7-in. skillet*

**SERVES 4**

These wraps are a cross between a pancake and an omelette. You can use any smoked fish for this, but I like hot smoked fish as this dispenses with cooking it first. Salmon, mackerel and eel would all work just as well as the haddock I've used here. Make sure the avocado is soft and ripe and season it really well.

Preheat the oven to low.

Gently beat the eggs in a bowl and season with salt and pepper. Put an ovenproof plate in the oven to heat up.

Heat about 1 teaspoon of the butter in the skillet over high heat and swirl it around the skillet. Pour in about 3 tablespoons of the beaten eggs—just enough to coat the base of the skillet. Wait for 30 seconds, then flip over. Repeat with the remaining mixture, using the same amount of butter each time, until you have about 8 omelets, keeping them warm on the plate in the oven.

Meanwhile, place the smoked haddock, watercress, avocado, and radishes in a large mixing bowl. Stir in the oil and lemon juice and season with pepper.

Lay 2 omelets out on a board and spoon some of the haddock filling down the middle of each one, then roll up and transfer to a plate. Repeat with the remaining wraps and 3 more plates.

*Smoked haddock, radish, & avocado omelet wraps (left)*

# Tortilla with potatoes, chiles, & piquillo peppers

6 tablespoons olive oil

1¼ lbs. (about 4) potatoes, peeled and thinly sliced

2 red chiles, thinly sliced

1 onion, thinly sliced

½ teaspoon sea salt

8 eggs

4 oz. jarred roasted piquillo peppers, drained and sliced

*an 8-in. nonstick skillet, at least 3 in. deep*

**SERVES 6**

The secret of a good tortilla (Spanish omelet) is to soften the potatoes in olive oil and then add them to the eggs and back into the skillet, not the other way round. If you pour the eggs directly into the skillet, they will not coat the potatoes evenly and you will get air bubbles. Don't rush the cooking either—the egg proteins will get agitated, resulting in a tough texture rather than a creamy finish.

Heat 4 tablespoons of the oil in the skillet, then add the potatoes, chiles, onion, and salt. Reduce the heat to low and cover with a lid. Cook for 15 minutes, stirring occasionally so the onions don't stick to the base of the pan.

Preheat the broiler.

Beat the eggs in a large mixing bowl. Transfer the cooked ingredients from the skillet to the beaten eggs and stir. Add the roasted peppers.

Turn the heat up to medium under the skillet and add the remaining oil. Pour the egg mixture into the skillet. Cook for 4–5 minutes until the base is golden—loosen the sides and lift up to check.

Broil for 3–4 minutes, until cooked all the way through. Cut into wedges.

# Wild mushroom mini-frittatas with garlic sourdough croutons

½ cup grated Parmesan, plus extra for dusting

1 oz. dried porcini mushrooms

2 tablespoons butter

3 shallots, finely chopped

2 garlic cloves, crushed

10 oz. wild mushrooms, such as chanterelles and trompettes

leaves from 2 sprigs of fresh thyme

8 eggs

sea salt and freshly ground black pepper

watercress, to serve

**CROUTONS**

2 slices of sourdough, torn into 1-in. chunks, crust and all

¼ cup olive oil

1 garlic clove, crushed

*a 9-cup muffin pan with large molds*

**MAKES 9**

**Frittatas look so cute when they are baked in individual muffin molds. Make this at the end of the summer when wild mushrooms are cheap and plentiful. The sourdough croutons add a good contrast in texture.**

Preheat the oven to 375°F. Grease the muffin pan and dust with Parmesan. Put the porcini in a little bowl with 2 tablespoons boiling water and let soak for 15 minutes.

To make the croutons, put the sourdough on a roasting pan, toss with the oil, garlic, and seasoning, and roast in the preheated oven for 20 minutes.

Melt the butter in a skillet, then add the shallots and sauté over low heat for 5–6 minutes, until softened. Add the garlic and wild mushrooms, turn up the heat, and cook for 3–4 minutes, until they become tender and any moisture has evaporated. Season well and add the thyme. Gently beat the eggs in a mixing bowl. Drain the soaked porcini and add to the eggs with the cooked ingredients from the skillet, the Parmesan, and some seasoning and beat. Divide between the muffin molds, dust with more Parmesan, and cook in the preheated oven for 18–20 minutes, until just set.

Let stand for 5 minutes, then serve with watercress and the croutons.

# pastries
# & breads

Walnut bread with goat cheese, honey, & wet walnuts  Easy sourdough bread  **Chile & cheddar cornbread**  Lemon & raisin soda bread Chocolate chip banana bread  **Marmalade & almond bread**  Crumpets Poppyseed bagels  **Sticky cinnamon & cardamom palmiers**  Jam & frangipane brioches  Dairy-free banana, date, & bran muffins  **Exploding berry crumble muffins**  Sugary jam donut muffins  Chocolate chip & peanut butter muffins  **Brioche french toast with pineapple & syrup** Apple streusel coffee cake  Maple pecan sticky buns  **Churros with cinnamon sugar**  Apple turnovers

# Walnut bread with goat cheese, honey, & wet walnuts

In fall when wet (fresh) walnuts abound, this is the most delicious way to serve them. The bread is quite sweet so it makes a lovely breakfast treat with chalky fresh goat cheese and a bowl of wet walnuts. I like to serve these in their shells, which forces people to interact with the food and heightens the enjoyment.

⅓ cup honey, plus extra
    to serve
1 envelope dried active
    yeast
2 cups hand-hot water
6½ tablespoons butter,
    melted
¼ cup walnut oil
1¼ cups shelled dried
    walnuts, chopped
1 tablespoon sea salt
4 cups whole-wheat flour
1½ cups bread flour,
    plus extra for dusting
13 oz. fresh goat cheese,
    to serve
a handful of wet (fresh)
    walnuts, or dried,
    to serve
*2 baking sheets,
    dusted with flour*
**MAKES 2 X 1-LB. LOAVES**

Put the honey, yeast, and water in a large bowl. Set aside in a draft-free place for 15 minutes until foamy on the surface. Pour in the butter, oil, walnuts, and salt.

Place the flour in a food mixer with a dough hook attachment. Alternatively, do this by hand. Set the mixer to the lowest speed and stir in the foamy mixture. The dough should be soft and slightly sticky. Turn the mixer up (or use elbow grease!) and knead the dough for 10–15 minutes. Place in a clean, lightly oiled bowl, cover with plastic wrap, and leave in a warm place for 1 hour, or until doubled in size.

Gently push the air out of the dough and take it out of the bowl, keeping the top as untouched as possible as this will be the structure of your crust. Slice the dough in half, shape into ovals, and smooth the edges by drawing the rough edges underneath and pinching them together on the underside. The top should be smooth and slightly stretched. Transfer to the prepared baking sheets, cover with a kitchen towel, and set aside for 20–30 minutes, until doubled in size. Preheat the oven to 450°F.

Dust the bread generously with flour and score the top with diagonal lines. Sprinkle the sides of the oven with a little water. Bake the bread in the preheated oven for 5 minutes, then reduce the heat to 400°F and bake for a further 25–30 minutes, until golden brown and hollow-sounding when tapped underneath. Let cool on a wire rack.

# Easy sourdough bread

3¼ cups rye flour

2 teaspoons sea salt

¾ cup hand-hot water

¾ oz. fresh yeast or
   1 tablespoon dried
   active yeast

2 cups whole-wheat flour

2 cups bread flour,
   plus extra for dusting

2 baking sheets,
   dusted with flour

**MAKES 2 X 1-LB. LOAVES**

**Real sourdough takes several days of commitment; as in the method below, you make a starter from flour and water and leave it until it begins to ferment and give off a tangy, alcoholic aroma. However, from here, you have to feed the starter to encourage the yeast to multiply. I have skipped this stage and just added the starter to the bread dough so that you get the tangy flavor without the wait.**

To make the starter, put 1¼ cups of the rye flour, the salt, and water in a large bowl. Cover with plastic wrap and leave at room temperature for 36 hours, by which time it should smell slightly tangy.

When you are ready to start making the dough, blend the yeast with ¾ cup hand-hot water (crumble it in if it is fresh yeast or sprinkle if it is dried). Transfer the remaining rye flour, and the whole-wheat and bread flours to a food mixer with a dough hook attachment. Alternatively, do this by hand. Set the mixer to the lowest speed and stir in the yeast mixture, followed by the sourdough starter, adding a little more warm water if it is still dry to achieve a soft, slightly sticky dough.

Turn the mixer up (or use some elbow grease!) and knead the dough for 10–15 minutes. Place in a clean, lightly oiled bowl, cover with plastic wrap, and leave in a warm place for 1–2 hours, until it has almost doubled in size.

Gently push the air out of the dough and take it out of the bowl, keeping the top as untouched as possible as this will be the structure of your crust. Slice the dough in half and smooth the edges by drawing the rough edges underneath and pinching them together on the underside. The top should be smooth and slightly stretched, and the loaf round. Transfer to the prepared baking sheets, cover with a kitchen towel, and set aside for 1 hour, until doubled in size. Meanwhile, preheat the oven to 450°F.

Dust the bread generously with flour and score the top with a criss-cross pattern. Sprinkle the sides of the oven with a little water. Bake the bread in the preheated oven for 5 minutes, then reduce the heat to 400°F and bake for a further 25–30 minutes, until golden brown and hollow-sounding when tapped underneath. Let cool on a wire rack.

# Chile & cheddar cornbread

1¼ cups all-purpose flour

2 teaspoons baking soda

1 teaspoon sea salt

1 cup medium cornmeal

2 tablespoons sugar

2 jalapeño chiles, chopped

1¼ cups grated sharp
  cheddar cheese, grated

1¼ cups buttermilk

3 tablespoons butter,
  melted

1 egg, beaten

*a 9-in. round or 8-in. square
cake pan, greased*

**SERVES 6–8**

Cornbread is not really a bread at all but a crumbly, buttery cake which can be served with fried chicken, or buttered and eaten for breakfast with a strong black coffee. It makes a nice change next to a plate of baked beans too, especially if they're homemade, such as the ones on page 128.

Preheat the oven to 375°F.

Sift the flour and baking soda into a mixing bowl and stir in the salt, cornmeal, sugar, chiles, and cheese.

In another bowl, beat together the buttermilk, butter, and egg. Pour into the dry ingredients and briefly fold in until no floury pockets remain. Scrape into the prepared cake pan and bake in the preheated oven for 20–25 minutes, until a skewer inserted into the center comes out clean. Let cool in the pan for 5 minutes, then turn out onto a wire rack to cool completely.

# Lemon & raisin soda bread

1 cup raisins

2 cups whole-wheat flour,
  plus extra for dusting

1 cup all-purpose flour

2 teaspoons baking soda

2 tablespoons sugar

1 teaspoon sea salt

1 cup buttermilk

finely grated zest of
  1 unwaxed lemon

*a baking sheet, lightly floured*

*a 9-in. round cake pan*

**SERVES 6–8**

This soda bread is studded with raisins and streaked with lemon zest, making it even more delicious than plain soda bread. It is one of the easiest breads to make because it requires no yeast, using baking soda as a raising agent. I like to toast it, slather it with butter, and eat it with one of the preserves in the last chapter of this book.

Preheat the oven to 425°F.

Soak the raisins in ¾ cup water for 15 minutes.

Put the flour, baking soda, sugar, and salt in a large mixing bowl. Make a well in the center and pour in the buttermilk, raisins, and their water, gradually drawing in the floury mixture with a wooden spoon until you have a soft, slightly loose but not sticky dough.

Bring the dough together with your hands and shape into a round roughly 9 inches across and 2 inches deep. Don't knead the dough or overwork it as you would with a yeasted bread—use a light touch as you would when making scones.

Place on the prepared baking sheet and score a large cross across the surface of the bread with a sharp knife. Dust with flour. Place the cake pan, upturned, on top of the bread to prevent it from browning too much. Bake in the preheated oven for 15 minutes.

Reduce the heat to 400°F, remove the cake pan from on top of the bread, and bake for a further 10–15 minutes, until it is hollow-sounding when tapped underneath. Let cool on a wire rack.

*Chile & cheddar cornbread (right)*

# Chocolate chip banana bread

1¾ cups all-purpose flour

1 teaspoon baking powder

½ teaspoon salt

¾ cup packed light
  brown sugar

4 overripe bananas, mashed

5½ tablespoons butter,
  melted

2 extra-large eggs, lightly
  beaten

⅔ cup chocolate chips

*a 9 x 5 x 3-in. loaf pan,
  greased and baselined
  with parchment paper*

**SERVES 8–10**

This is a cake that can't go wrong, unless you are not patient enough to wait for the bananas to ripen. This is a real no-no; they have to be black to get that deep flavor. In fact, in our house, we make this loaf to suit the look of our bananas, not the other way round. Saying that, we seem to let them go black a lot more than we need to, in anticipation of this cake. The chocolate chips are just gilding the lily but when they come out molten and oozy it makes the loaf irresistible.

Preheat the oven to 350°F.

Put the flour, baking powder, and salt in a mixing bowl. In another bowl, mix the sugar and bananas until there are no large lumps. Beat in the butter and eggs.

Tip the wet ingredients into the dry ingredients and mix, being careful not to overmix otherwise the loaf will be tough. Stir in the chocolate chips. Spoon the batter into the prepared loaf pan and bake on the center shelf of the preheated oven for 40–45 minutes, until a skewer inserted into the center comes out clean.

Let the loaf cool in the pan for 10 minutes, then turn out onto a wire rack to cool completely. When cold, serve in slices with butter or a decadent dollop of ricotta.

# Marmalade & almond bread

**This fragrant quick bread is streaked with zesty marmalade and kept moist by the addition of ground almonds. Be careful not to bake this in a very hot oven as the sugar content is high and the outside likes to brown. Serve it in chunky slices with Earl Grey tea.**

2 sticks butter, softened

¾ cup sugar

freshly squeezed juice of
½ orange

finely grated zest of
1 orange

½ cup orange marmalade

4 extra-large eggs

1 cup plus 2 tablespoons
self-rising flour

½ cup ground almonds

*a 9 x 5 x 3-in. loaf pan,
greased and baselined
with parchment paper*

**SERVES 8–10**

Preheat the oven to 325°F.

Put the butter and sugar in a large mixing bowl and beat with an electric handheld whisk until the mixture is pale and light. Gradually add the orange juice, zest, and the marmalade and swirl through with the whisk.

Lightly beat the eggs with a fork in a small bowl. Keep the electric whisk running in the creamed butter bowl and trickle the eggs in, 1 tablespoon at a time, beating thoroughly after each addition to stop them curdling. Finally, fold in the flour and ground almonds. Spoon the mixture into the prepared loaf pan and bake on a low shelf in the preheated oven for about 45 minutes, until lightly golden on top. A skewer inserted in the middle should come out clean.

Let the bread cool in the pan for 15 minutes, then transfer to a wire rack to cool completely. It is easier to slice when it's cold—if you can resist its alluring aroma while it cools.

# Crumpets

2 cups whole milk

I teaspoon sugar

$^{3}/_{4}$ oz. fresh yeast or
  I tablespoon dried
  active yeast

I$^{1}/_{2}$ cups bread flour

I$^{1}/_{2}$ cups all-purpose flour

I teaspoon salt

2 tablespoons sunflower
  oil

I cup hand-hot water

$^{1}/_{2}$ teaspoon baking soda

*4 x 3-in. metal rings, greased*

**MAKES 12**

**Making English crumpets is like going back to the childhood days of chemistry sets—you may not understand the chemical reaction happening, but it's great to see the crumpets bubble, ready to receive melted butter in their pockets.**

Pour the milk and sugar into a saucepan and heat until hand-hot. Remove from the heat, scatter over the yeast, and set aside for 10 minutes until foamy on the surface.

Sift the flours and salt into a mixing bowl and add the wet, foamy mixture. Beat with an electric handheld whisk for a good 2–3 minutes, until smooth. Cover with plastic wrap and leave in a draft-free place for 1$^{1}/_{2}$–2 hours, until it has doubled in size and is covered in tiny bubbles.

Mix the water and baking soda until dissolved. Using the electric whisk, beat this into the risen dough until smooth. Cover again and let rise for a further 20 minutes.

Put the metal rings on a hot nonstick skillet. Spoon 2 tablespoons of the batter into each ring so they are half full. Cook over very low heat for 5–7 minutes until the surface is pockmarked and dry around the edges. Slide the rings off, flip the crumpets over, and cook for 1 minute, until pale gold. Wrap in a clean kitchen towel while you cook the rest. Serve with butter and a big pot of raspberry jam.

# Poppyseed bagels

I envelope dried active
  yeast

$^{1}/_{4}$ cup honey

I$^{1}/_{4}$ cups hand-hot water

3$^{1}/_{2}$ cups bread flour

I teaspoon salt

2 teaspoons baking soda

2 tablespoons poppyseeds

*a baking sheet, lined with
  parchment paper*

**MAKES 10**

**Moist chewy bagels are made from a fairly standard white dough, but they are poached before being baked. I like to smother them in cream cheese and excessive amounts of raspberry jam for that sweet and savory contrast.**

Put the yeast in a small bowl with the honey and $^{1}/_{2}$ cup of the water. Set aside for 10 minutes until frothy.

Put the flour and salt in a bowl and make a well in the center. Pour in the frothy mixture and draw the flour into the liquid with a wooden spoon. Add more hand-hot water and continue to mix until you get a soft dough. It should not be very sticky. Turn out onto a lightly floured surface and knead for 10 minutes. Return to the bowl, cover, and leave in a draft-free place for 20 minutes.

Divide the dough into 10 equal pieces. Shape each piece into a flattish ball, then take a wooden spoon and use the handle to make a hole in the middle of each ball. Twirl the bagel around the spoon to make a hole 1$^{1}/_{2}$ inches wide. It will close up on cooking, so exaggerate it. Lay the bagels on the baking sheet and cover. Set aside for 30–45 minutes.

Preheat the oven to 450°F.

Bring a large pan of salted water to a boil and add the baking soda. Poach 3 bagels at a time for 30 seconds on each side. Fish out, drain off any excess water, and scatter with poppyseeds. Place on the baking sheet. Bake for 10 minutes until lightly golden and baked through.

*Crumpets (right)*

# Sticky cinnamon & cardamom palmiers

6 cardamom pods

6 tablespoons demerara
    sugar

1 teaspoon ground
    cinnamon

¼ cup poppyseeds

12 oz. puff pastry dough,
    thawed if frozen

1 egg, beaten

*a nonstick baking sheet*

**MAKES 16**

**These little sugary pastries are ideal as a mid-morning snack with a strong black coffee. You can vary the spices or omit the cardamom and leave them plain.**

Preheat the oven to 400°F.

Put the cardamom pods in a freezer bag and crush them to separate the pale green husks from the black seeds inside. Discard the husks and crush the seeds with the sugar using a pestle and mortar, just until they break up a little. Transfer to a small bowl with the ground cinnamon and poppyseeds.

Roll out the pastry on a lightly floured work surface into a rectangle approximately 24 x 12 inches. Brush all over with the beaten egg and scatter half the dry ingredients over the top. Fold the two shorter edges over to meet in the middle. Brush with more egg wash and scatter with the remaining dry ingredients. Bring the new outside ends over again to join in the middle. Fold the pastry in half as if you were closing a book. Lift onto the nonstick baking sheet, then gently press down so you have a rectangular log with pleated folds. Chill in the refrigerator for 30 minutes to firm up before slicing.

Remove from the refrigerator and cut into ½-inch slices. Return each slice, flat side down, to the baking sheet with some room to expand. Bake in the preheated oven for 18–20 minutes, until golden. Let cool on a wire rack.

## Jam & frangipane brioches

These are a are a little like an old French recipe for using up stale brioche, called Bostock. They are surprisingly easy to whip up and are wonderful for a decadent breakfast. They will keep for a couple of days and can be polished off at teatime or warmed and eaten with cream for dessert.

5 tablespoons unsalted
   butter, softened

⅓ cup sugar

1 egg yolk

½ cup ground almonds

⅓ cup raspberry, rhubarb,
   or apricot jam

6 stale brioche fingers
   or 4 stale brioche buns,
   halved

3 tablespoons flaked
   almonds

*a baking sheet, lined with
   parchment paper*

**MAKES 8–12**

Preheat the oven to 375°F.

To make what is effectively frangipane, put the butter and sugar in a bowl and beat with an electric handheld whisk until light and fluffy. Beat in the egg yolk in 2 stages (so that it doesn't curdle), then fold in the ground almonds.

Spread the jam over the cut sides of the brioche, then spread a blob of frangipane on top. Scatter with the flaked almonds. Transfer to the prepared baking sheet and bake in the preheated oven for 10–12 minutes, until the topping is puffed up and tinged with brown.

# Dairy-free banana, date, & bran muffins

1 cup plus 2 tablespoons
   whole-wheat flour

2/3 cup plus 2 tablespoons
   wheat bran

a pinch of salt

2 teaspoons ground
   cinnamon

2 teaspoons baking powder

2 eggs

1/3 cup honey

3/4 cup soy milk

1/3 cup vegetable oil

1 cup pitted dates, chopped

3 bananas, sliced

*a 12-cup muffin pan*

**MAKES 10–12**

**These muffins are full of fiber and super filling. As with all muffins, they need to be stirred with a hand that is not too worried about getting every last lump out, as this rocky batter gives them their characteristically clumpy, rough texture.**

Preheat the oven to 350°F. Line the muffin pan with paper cases.

Sift the flour, 2/3 cup of the wheat bran, the salt, cinnamon, and baking powder into a large mixing bowl.

Beat the eggs with the honey, soy milk, and oil. Pour the wet ingredients into the dry ingredients and scatter the dates and bananas on top. Using a large spoon, fold until the mixture is moistened. It needs to be lumpy and shouldn't be overworked otherwise the baked muffins will be tough. Spoon into the paper cases until they are two-thirds full and scatter over the reserved bran. Bake in the preheated oven for 18–22 minutes.

Let cool in the pan for 5 minutes before transferring to a wire rack.

# Exploding berry crumble muffins

2 3/4 cups all-purpose flour

1 tablespoon baking
   powder

1 teaspoon baking soda

3/4 cup sugar

1/2 teaspoon salt

2 eggs, beaten

1 stick unsalted butter,
   melted

3/4 cup sour cream

1/4 cup whole milk

1 1/4 cups raspberries

**TOPPING**

3/4 cup all-purpose flour

5 tablespoons butter,
   chilled and cubed

2 tablespoons coarse sugar

3 tablespoons slivered
   almonds

*a 12-cup muffin pan*

**MAKES 12**

**These look like the muffins which are sold in cafés and which seem to have exploded out of their pans with their generous proportions. There is no secret trick to this—just fill the muffin cases up to the top.**

Preheat the oven to 375°F. Line the muffin pan with paper cases and grease the surface of the pan where the muffins will rise and stick.

To make the topping, put the flour and butter in a food processor and pulse briefly, just until the butter is blended. Tip out into a bowl and add the sugar and almonds, pressing the mixture together with your hands.

To make the muffins, sift the flour, baking powder, baking soda, sugar, and salt into a large mixing bowl. Break the eggs into a large glass measuring cup, add the melted butter, sour cream, and milk, and whisk to combine. Pour the wet ingredients into the dry ingredients and scatter the raspberries on top. Using a large spoon, fold until the mixture is moistened. It needs to be lumpy and shouldn't be overworked otherwise the muffins will be tough. Spoon into the paper cases right to the top. For regular-size (not exploding!) muffins you can spoon the cases two-thirds full—you will be able to make more of these with this amount of mixture. Finish by scattering over the topping. Bake in the preheated oven for 25–28 minutes for large muffins, or 18–22 minutes for the smaller ones.

Let cool for 5 minutes in the pan before transferring to a wire rack.

*Exploding berry crumble muffins (right)*

# Sugary jam donut muffins

1/3 cup sunflower oil

2/3 cup plain yogurt

1/2 teaspoon vanilla extract

2 extra-large eggs, beaten

2 cups plus 2 tablespoons
    self-rising flour

1/2 teaspoon baking soda

a pinch of salt

1/2 cup sugar

1/3 cup blueberry jam

**TOPPING**

2 tablespoons unsalted
    butter, melted

1/4 cup sugar

*a 6-cup muffin pan,
    lined with paper cases*

**MAKES 6**

This is a recipe for anyone who likes a warm sugary donut but dislikes the deep frying involved in making them. Of course, the result is more cakey than bready but they are every bit as delicious, as they ooze jam and cover your lips with sugar crystals.

Preheat the oven to 375°F.

Put the oil, yogurt, vanilla, and eggs in a bowl and beat together.

In another, large bowl, mix together the flour, baking soda, salt, and sugar. Pour the wet ingredients into the dry ingredients and swiftly mix together, until just combined. It needs to be quite lumpy but you need to hassle any floury pockets until there are no more.

Drop 1 heaping tablespoon of the batter in each paper case. Make a dip in the mixture and spoon in a heaping teaspoon of the jam. Divide the remaining batter between the paper cases to cover the jam. Bake in the preheated oven for 18–20 minutes, until well risen. Set aside, still in the pan, to cool for 5 minutes before you apply the topping.

When the muffins have cooled for 5 minutes, brush their tops with the melted butter for the topping and roll in the sugar. Transfer to a wire rack to cool to room temperature.

# Chocolate chip & peanut butter muffins

2 cups all-purpose flour

2 teaspoons baking powder

1/2 teaspoon baking soda

1/3 cup sugar

1 cup crunchy peanut
    butter

1 extra-large egg, beaten

3 1/2 tablespoons butter,
    melted

1/2 cup plain yogurt

1/3 cup whole milk

2/3 cup milk chocolate
    chips

*a 12-cup muffin pan,
    lined with paper cases*

**MAKES 12**

You can't really go wrong with salty peanuts and sweet chocolate. If you love Reese's Pieces, then this is the muffin you've been waiting for. For these indulgent muffins, I prefer the creamy sweetness of milk chocolate, rather than the more refined bittersweet chocolate I usually use for baking.

Preheat the oven to 350°F.

Sift the flour, baking powder, and baking soda into a large mixing bowl, then add the sugar and crunchy peanut butter.

Put the egg, melted butter, yogurt, and milk in a bowl and beat together. Stir in the chocolate chips. Pour the wet ingredients into the dry ingredients. Using a large spoon, fold until the mixture is moistened. It needs to be lumpy and shouldn't be overworked otherwise the muffins will be tough. Spoon into the paper cases until they are two-thirds full. Bake in the preheated oven for 20–22 minutes, until golden and well risen.

Let cool in the pan for 5 minutes before transferring to a wire rack.

*Sugary jam donut muffins (left)*

# Brioche french toast with pineapple & syrup

1 vanilla bean, split
   lengthwise
$\frac{1}{2}$ cup packed light
   brown sugar
2 cinnamon sticks
6 eggs, beaten
6 tablespoons whole milk
8 thick slices of brioche
   loaf
2 tablespoons butter
3 tablespoons sunflower
   oil
1 pineapple, peeled, cored,
   and sliced into rounds
**SERVES 4**

**Light, buttery brioche makes wonderful French toast. As it is so rich, a slightly tart fruit is needed—I like to grill slices of pineapple and drench them in syrup.**

Scrape the seeds out of the vanilla bean. Put half the seeds, the bean, the sugar, $\frac{3}{4}$ cup water, and the cinnamon in a saucepan over low heat and heat gently until the sugar has dissolved. Turn up the heat and simmer for 10 minutes, until syrupy. Meanwhile, put the eggs, milk, and remaining vanilla seeds in a wide bowl and whisk together lightly. Dip the brioche in the egg mixture, transfer to a plate, and set aside to soak up all the mixture.

Heat half the butter and oil in your largest skillet over medium heat. Add as many slices of soaked bread as you can and cook for 2–3 minutes on each side. Repeat until all the bread is fried.

Heat a stovetop grill pan over high heat and brush the pineapple with a little of the syrup. Grill for 2 minutes on each side. Serve 2 slices of French toast with a couple of slices of pineapple and a drizzle of the syrup.

# Apple streusel coffee cake

10 tablespoons butter,
   softened
$\frac{3}{4}$ cup sugar
2 extra-large eggs, beaten
2 teaspoons vanilla extract
$\frac{3}{4}$ cup all-purpose flour
$\frac{1}{2}$ teaspoon baking powder
$\frac{1}{2}$ teaspoon baking soda
$\frac{2}{3}$ cup ground almonds
$\frac{1}{2}$ cup sour cream
3 apples, peeled, cored,
   and thinly sliced

**TOPPING**
$\frac{2}{3}$ cup all-purpose flour
$\frac{1}{3}$ cup light brown sugar
$\frac{1}{2}$ teaspoon ground
   cinnamon
3 tablespoons butter
$\frac{2}{3}$ cup chopped pecans
*an 8-in. round cake pan*
**SERVES 8**

**This is a coffee cake in the sense that it is good with a mid-morning coffee. The cake mixture is really vanillary and stays a little bit moist around the apples as they let off their steam. I adore the contrast of this against the nutty, crunchy topping. A strong coffee and a gossip are all you need to accessorize this delight.**

Preheat the oven to 350°F. Line the cake pan with parchment paper.

Cream the butter and sugar with an electric handheld whisk until fluffy. Gradually beat in the eggs and vanilla, then fold in the flour, baking powder, baking soda, and almonds. Beat in the sour cream until you have a dropping consistency. Spoon half the batter into the prepared pan. Arrange the apples snugly on top, in a single layer, and spoon over the remaining batter.

To make the topping, put the flour, sugar, and cinnamon in a bowl and rub in the butter with your fingertips until the mixture is crumbly. Add 1 tablespoon water and the pecans and break into lumps with a blunt knife. Scatter this over the cake and bake in the preheated oven for 50–60 minutes. A skewer inserted in the middle of the cake should come out clean. If it doesn't, bake for a few minutes more before checking again (noting that the apples will make it seem quite wet).

Let the cake cool in the pan for 10 minutes, then transfer to a wire rack to cool completely. Alternatively, enjoy it with cream while it is still warm.

*Apple streusel coffee cake (right)*

# Maple pecan sticky buns

1 cup whole milk,
    plus extra for glazing

6 tablespoons unsalted
    butter

3¾ cups bread flour

¼ cup packed light
    brown sugar

1 envelope rapid-rise
    dried yeast

½ teaspoon salt

1 egg, beaten

**FILLING**

5 tablespoons unsalted
    butter, softened

⅓ cup pure maple syrup

⅓ cup packed light
    brown sugar

1 tablespoon ground
    cinnamon

⅔ cup chopped pecans

**MAKES ABOUT 16**

It's quite fun to make your own sticky buns, but you need to start the day before unless you are a hopeless insomniac. This dough is enriched with butter and egg and is ready to bake when it is like a soft, puffy marshmallow. Try putting different nuts, chocolate chips, and/or dried fruit in the center for a change. They are best served warm on the day they are made, so if you are eating them after that, warm them a little in the oven first to soften up.

Put the milk and butter in a saucepan and heat gently until the butter has melted. Remove from the heat and let cool slightly. Put the flour, sugar, yeast, and salt in a large bowl.

Pour the egg into the cooled milk and beat. Make a well in the center of the dry ingredients and pour in the milk mixture. Gradually draw in the floury mixture with a wooden spoon until it is all combined. Bring the dough together with your hands, then tip out onto a lightly floured work surface and knead for 10 minutes, until smooth and the dough springs back when poked. Place in a lightly oiled bowl and cover with plastic wrap. Let rise for 1–2 hours.

Meanwhile, to make the filling, mix the butter, maple syrup, sugar, and cinnamon in a small bowl and set aside.

Push the air out of the dough and lay it on the work surface. Using the heel of your hand, flatten and shape it into a rectangle about 12 x 16 inches. Spread the filling over the surface of the dough. With one of the long sides facing you, roll up the dough like a jelly roll and chill in the refrigerator for 1 hour.

Cut the roll into ¾-inch slices. Arrange these, flat side down, on a baking sheet spaced about 1 inch apart so that they have room to expand. Cover loosely with plastic wrap and let rise for 30 minutes, until puffy.

Preheat the oven to 400°F.

Brush the buns with milk and slide into the preheated oven. Immediately reduce the heat to 350°F and bake for 12–15 minutes, until baked through and golden.

## Churros with cinnamon sugar

3 tablespoons butter
2 tablespoons sugar
1 cup all-purpose flour
a pinch of salt
2 extra-large eggs, beaten
about 3 cups vegetable oil,
    for deep frying

**CINNAMON SUGAR**
6 tablespoons sugar
1 teaspoon ground
    cinnamon
*a piping bag, fitted with*
    *a ½-in. star tip*
**MAKES 12**

**These Spanish morsels of deliciousness are a bit like donuts. Making them is a little like making French choux pastry, except that the batter is then squeezed out of a piping bag into boiling hot oil. I know this all sounds like a labor of love but there is nothing better on a rainy day than to enjoy them with a cup of hot chocolate. When they cool down, they lose a lot of their magic.**

Put the butter, sugar, and ⅔ cup water in a small saucepan and bring to a boil. Tip the flour and salt into the boiling water, remove from the heat, and beat vigorously with a wooden spoon for 20 seconds, until the mixture comes away from the sides of the pan and forms a clump. Let cool for 10 minutes or until it is lukewarm.

Beat in the eggs, a spoonful at a time. Cover, chill in the refrigerator, and let cool completely.

Fill a large saucepan one-third full with vegetable oil. Heat to 375°F (or until a dot of the churros batter bubbles up and floats straightaway). Spoon the batter into the prepared piping bag. Squeeze 3 x 3½-inch lengths of batter into the hot oil. (Use your finger to release the batter from the tip of the piping bag.) Fry for 2 minutes on each side until golden. Drain on paper towels and fry the remaining batter in the same way.

To make the cinnamon sugar, mix the sugar and cinnamon in a large, wide dish. Roll the churros in the mixture while they are hot and oily, until evenly coated. Serve with hot chocolate or coffee.

# Apple turnovers

2 tablespoons unsalted
butter
½ cup demerara sugar
2 McIntosh or other
fragrant apples, peeled,
cored, and chopped
¼ teaspoon ground nutmeg
½ teaspoon ground
cinnamon
finely grated zest of
1 unwaxed lemon
1 tablespoon freshly
squeezed lemon juice
12 oz. puff pastry dough,
thawed if frozen
1 egg yolk mixed with
1 tablespoon milk
*a baking sheet, lightly dusted
with flour*

**MAKES 6**

These are quick to whip up. You can even use a storebought spiced apple sauce for a cheat's version. If you are lucky enough to know someone who has a McIntosh apple tree, you would be doing them a favor to make use of their windfall, so reserve this recipe for the fall, for times such as these.

Preheat the oven to 400°F.

Put the butter and 5 tablespoons of the sugar in a saucepan over medium heat and leave until the butter has melted. Add the apples, nutmeg, cinnamon, and lemon zest and juice. Cover with a lid and stir occasionally for 3–4 minutes, until the apple pieces gracefully collapse into a chunky purée. Set aside to cool slightly.

Roll out the pastry on a lightly floured work surface until it is ¼ inch thick. Trim any curvy edges into straight lines, then cut into about 6 x 4-inch squares.

Spoon a dollop of the apple purée in the center of each pastry square.

Brush the edges with egg wash. Fold over one corner so it meets with the other and press gently. Crimp the edges with a fork or your fingers to seal in the filling. Using a sharp knife, slit the top 4 or 5 times to allow the steam to escape and stop the pastry going soggy. Transfer the turnovers to the prepared baking sheet and glaze with egg wash. Sprinkle the remaining sugar over the top. Bake in the preheated oven for 20 minutes, until golden and puffed up.

Let cool for just a few moments before devouring (without burning your mouth on the hot filling!), or eat cold.

# pancakes & waffles

Potato & rosemary pancakes with bacon & honey  Buckwheat crêpes with mushrooms, caramelized onions, bacon, & gruyère  **Blinis with smoked salmon & crème fraîche**  Sweet potato pancakes with smoked trout & chile-lime butter  Orange cornmeal hotcakes with orange flower syrup  **Blueberry pancakes**  Apricot pancakes with maple & pecan butter  Lemon ricotta pancakes with blackberries  **Buckwheat & banana pancakes**  Dairy-free coconut pancakes with lime syrup & mango  Buttermilk waffles with crème fraîche, bitter chocolate sauce, & hazelnuts  **Gingerbread waffles with strawberries**

## Potato & rosemary pancakes with bacon & honey

1 lb. potatoes, peeled

1 tablespoon finely chopped
fresh rosemary needles

1 cup plus 2 tablespoons
all-purpose flour

½ teaspoon baking soda

1 cup plus 2 tablespoons
buttermilk

12 bacon slices

2 tablespoons butter

sea salt and freshly ground
black pepper

honey, to serve

**SERVES 4**

These pancakes are based on the Irish potato dish called boxty, in which some of the potatoes are cooked and mashed, and the others are grated to give the pancakes a bit of texture on top of the fluffiness. They were obviously once seen as a sign of domesticity, as they prompted the saying: "Boxty on the griddle, boxty in the pan, if you can't make boxty, you'll never get a man."

Put a generous half of the potatoes in a saucepan of cold, salted water and bring to a boil. Cook for 20–25 minutes, until soft. Drain and mash, then season and add the rosemary. Let cool.

Meanwhile, peel and grate the remaining potatoes and leave them raw. Put both sets of potato in a mixing bowl and beat in the flour and baking soda, then the buttermilk.

Preheat the broiler.

Cook the bacon under the broiler until well done (there's no need to turn it over while it's cooking). Let cool for 4–5 minutes, until crisp. Turn off the broiler and keep the bacon in a low oven while you continue cooking.

Heat half the butter in a skillet over low/medium heat and wait for it to sizzle. Drop 2–3 ladlefuls of the batter into the skillet, spaced apart, and spread out with a spatula. They need about 3 minutes on the first side, then a little less on the other side. Keep warm with the bacon in the oven while you cook the rest.

Serve 2–3 pancakes per person, with a few bacon slices and some honey to drizzle over.

# Buckwheat crêpes with mushrooms, caramelized onions, bacon, & gruyère

1/3 cup buckwheat flour

1/2 cup all-purpose flour

1 large egg

2/3 cup whole milk

sunflower oil, for frying

sea salt and freshly ground
black pepper

**FILLING**

2 tablespoons butter

2 large red onions, sliced

sprig of fresh thyme

6 1/2 oz. cremini
mushrooms, sliced

6 1/2 oz. thick-sliced bacon,
cubed

2 garlic cloves, sliced

2/3 cup grated Gruyère
cheese

2/3 cup crème fraîche

*a 9-in. skillet*

**SERVES 4**

**This is a classic combination from Normandy. Make sure your batter is thin enough to run over the skillet easily or you'll end up with crêpes that are not delicate and lacy, but thick and stodgy.**

Mix the flours and a large pinch of salt in a mixing bowl and make a well in the center. Beat the egg and milk in a small bowl, and pour into the flours. Gradually draw the flour into the liquid with a wooden spoon until smooth. Cover and chill in the fridge for 1 hour.

Preheat the oven to low.

Whisk 1/3 cup water into the rested batter—it should now be the consistency of light cream.

To make the filling, heat the butter in a skillet over low heat. Stir in the onions and thyme, season with black pepper, cover, and cook for 10 minutes, until the onion has softened. Turn up the heat and add the mushrooms, bacon, and garlic. Stir for 6–8 minutes, until lightly caramelized. Stir in the Gruyère and crème fraîche and remove from the heat.

Heat your 9-inch skillet over medium heat. Grease the skillet with a kitchen towel dipped in oil. Pour in 3 tablespoons of the batter, swirl to coat the base of the skillet, and cook for 1 minute on each side. Keep warm in the oven while you cook the rest.

Reheat the filling until bubbling and smooth (remove the thyme sprig), season, then divide between the crêpes.

# Blinis with smoked salmon & crème fraîche

1/3 cup buckwheat flour

1/2 cup bread flour

1 teaspoon salt

1/2 cup whole milk

1/3 cup crème fraîche,
plus extra to serve

1 teaspoon fresh yeast,
crumbled, or 1 envelope
dried active yeast

1 extra-large egg, separated

sunflower oil, for frying

smoked salmon, to serve

snipped chives (optional)

**MAKES 20 SMALL BLINIS**

**It's worth making your own fresh blinis because their flavor is much more complex than the ready-made kind. You can make the batter the night before, then let it have its final rising half an hour before cooking. They freeze well too.**

Sift the flours and salt into a large mixing bowl. Heat the milk in a saucepan until hand hot. Add the crème fraîche and yeast and stir until smooth. Pour onto the flours with the egg yolk and stir well to blend. Cover and let rise for 1 hour.

Beat the egg white with an electric handheld whisk until soft peaks form. Fold into the batter, cover, and leave for 30 minutes. Preheat the oven to low.

To make the blinis, heat a heavy-based skillet over medium heat. Grease with a kitchen towel dipped in oil. Drop in 2 tablespoons of the batter. After 30 seconds bubbles will appear on the surface. Flip the blini over and cook for 30 seconds on the other side. Keep warm in the oven while you cook the rest. Serve with crème fraîche, smoked salmon, chives, if using, and black pepper.

## Sweet potato pancakes with smoked trout & chile-lime butter

8 oz. sweet potato, peeled

3 tablespoons sunflower
   oil, plus extra for frying

1 cup whole milk

1 egg

1 cup all-purpose flour

2 teaspoons baking powder

a pinch of cayenne pepper

2 teaspoons fish sauce

8 oz. smoked trout

cilantro, to garnish

**CHILE-LIME BUTTER**

2 scallions, sliced

1 red chile, shredded

1 teaspoon grated fresh
   ginger

1 teaspoon demerara sugar

2 teaspoons fish sauce

freshly squeezed juice
   of 2 limes

5 tablespoons butter

**SERVES 4**

This makes a delicious Thai-inspired brunch dish. The sweet potato helps to keep the pancakes beautifully moist and using fish sauce instead of salt adds another Thai-style touch. The chile-lime butter soaks into the pancakes and really brings out the flavor of the sweet potato. Even if the dish sounds a little novel to you, try it because all the flavors work beautifully and it makes a change from the usual maple syrup and pancake combination.

Preheat the oven to low.

Halve the sweet potato and put in a saucepan of boiling water. Simmer for 25 minutes until really soft. Test with a knife to check it is evenly cooked.

Drain the potatoes and mash with the oil. Stir in the milk and let the mixture cool before beating in the egg. Sift in the flour, baking powder, and cayenne pepper, and season with the fish sauce instead of salt. Set aside.

To make the chile-lime butter, mix the scallions, chile, ginger, sugar, fish sauce, and lime juice and set aside.

Heat a skillet or griddle over medium heat. Grease the skillet with a kitchen towel dipped in oil. Drop in 2 tablespoons of the potato batter and cook for 2 minutes on the first side, until bubbles appear and the edges are dry. Flip over and cook on the other side for a further 2 minutes. Keep warm in the oven while you cook the rest.

Melt the butter for the chile-lime butter in a saucepan and stir in the reserved dressing. Serve the pancakes topped with trout and cilantro, and pour over the warm chile-lime butter.

# Orange cornmeal hotcakes with orange flower syrup

⅔ cup buttermilk

2 eggs, separated

3 tablespoons freshly
squeezed orange juice

finely grated zest of
½ orange

½ cup cornmeal

½ cup all-purpose flour

3 tablespoons brown sugar

1 teaspoon baking powder

a pinch of salt

melted butter, to serve

**ORANGE FLOWER SYRUP**

½ cup maple syrup

a drop of orange flower
water

**SERVES 4**

These pancakes have a citrusy tang to them and a slightly granular crunch from the cornmeal. The maple syrup is spiked with a small drop of fragrant orange flower water, but a little bit of butter on the hotcakes first won't go amiss.

Preheat the oven to low.

To make the orange flower syrup, stir the maple syrup and orange flower water together in a small bowl.

Put the buttermilk, egg yolks, orange juice, and zest in a mixing bowl and beat together. Add the cornmeal, flour, sugar, baking powder, and salt and fold in until just moistened. Do not overmix otherwise you will toughen the texture.

Whisk the egg whites in a separate bowl with an electric handheld whisk until soft peaks form. Using a large metal spoon, fold the whites into the batter.

Wipe a skillet with a kitchen towel dipped in melted butter. Heat up, then drop in 2–3 tablespoons of the batter. Cook for 2 minutes, until bubbles appear on the top and the edges are dry. Cook in batches of 3 or whatever fits comfortably in your skillet. Flip the hotcake over and cook for 2 minutes on the other side.

Serve about 3 hotcakes per person. Put some melted butter on each hotcake and serve with the orange flower syrup.

# Blueberry pancakes

1 cup self-rising flour

1 teaspoon baking powder

2 tablespoons sugar

¼ teaspoon salt

1 egg

⅓ cup whole milk

3 tablespoons butter,
melted

1 generous cup blueberries,
plus extra to serve

maple syrup, to serve

**SERVES 4**

Perfect blueberry pancakes should be light and fluffy, with a good rise on them. The secret is to use some water—an all-milk batter makes the pancakes heavier. And remember to serve them with lashings of maple syrup.

Preheat the oven to low.

Sift the flour and baking powder into a mixing bowl and stir in the sugar and salt. Put the egg, milk, and ⅓ cup water in a glass measuring cup and beat to blend.

Stir half the butter into the wet ingredients in the measuring cup. Mix the wet ingredients with the dry ingredients until no lumps of flour remain.

Wipe a heavy-based skillet with a scrunched-up kitchen towel dipped in the remaining melted butter. Heat up, then drop in ⅓ cup of the batter. Cook for 1–2 minutes on the first side, then scatter over a few of the blueberries and flip the pancake over. Cook for 2 minutes, until golden and cooked through. Keep warm in the oven while you make the rest.

Serve with more blueberries and lashings of maple syrup.

*Blueberry pancakes (left)*

# Apricot pancakes with maple & pecan butter

1 cup self-rising flour

1 teaspoon baking powder

2 tablespoons sugar

3 tablespoons butter,
    melted

¼ teaspoon salt

1 egg

⅔ cup whole milk

4 apricots, pitted and
    roughly chopped

**MAPLE & PECAN BUTTER**

3 tablespoons shelled
    pecans, chopped

5 tablespoons butter,
    softened

2 tablespoons pure
    maple syrup

**SERVES 4**

**Soft drupe fruits work beautifully with fluffy pancakes, but make sure they are really soft and ripe. Apricots are among my favorite fruit, with their sweet perfumed flesh and inoffensively furry skin.**

Preheat the oven to low.

To make the maple & pecan butter, put the pecans in a dry skillet over medium heat and let them heat up. Stir so they brown evenly, then remove from the heat.

Beat the butter and maple syrup together. It may take a while to come together but once it warms up enough it will blend smoothly. Stir in the toasted pecans and set aside.

Sift the flour and baking powder in a large mixing bowl and stir in the sugar and salt. Put half the butter, the egg, milk, and ⅓ cup water in a large glass measuring cup and beat to combine. Mix the wet ingredients with the dry ingredients until no lumps of flour remain.

Wipe a heavy-based skillet with a scrunched-up kitchen towel dipped in melted butter. Heat up, then drop in 2–3 tablespoons of batter on one side of the skillet and the same on the other side of the skillet Cook for about 1–2 minutes on the first side, until the edges look dry, then scatter over some apricots and flip over. Cook for 2 minutes, until golden and cooked through. Keep warm in the oven while you make the rest. Serve with the maple & pecan butter.

# Lemon ricotta pancakes with blackberries

1 cup ricotta

freshly squeezed juice
    and grated zest of
    1 unwaxed lemon

3 eggs, separated

3 tablespoons butter,
    melted

¾ cup all-purpose flour

1 teaspoon baking soda

a pinch of salt

4 tablespoons sugar

blackberries and crème
    fraîche, to serve

**SERVES 4**

**These pancakes are very fluffy and light. They need to cook slowly as they are so delicate. You can turn them into savory pancakes by omitting the sugar and folding through some chopped green herbs, such as chives and tarragon, then serving with smoked salmon instead of blackberries.**

Preheat the oven to low.

Put the ricotta, lemon juice and zest, egg yolks, and half the butter in a mixing bowl and beat together. Sift in the flour, baking soda, and salt and fold in. Whisk the egg whites in a separate bowl with an electric handheld whisk until soft peaks form. Add the sugar and whisk until glossy and firm. Using a large metal spoon, fold the whites into the batter.

Wipe a heavy-based skillet with a scrunched-up kitchen towel dipped in the melted butter. Drop a heaping tablespoon of batter in the skillet to make a 2½-inch circle. Cook in batches of 3 or 4 depending on the size of the skillet. Cook for 2 minutes on each side until risen and cooked through. Keep warm in the oven while you make the rest. Serve with blackberries and crème fraîche.

*Lemon ricotta pancakes with blackberries (right)*

# Buckwheat & banana pancakes

½ cup buckwheat flour

6 tablespoons all-purpose
flour

I teaspoon baking soda

¼ teaspoon salt

2 tablespoons honey,
plus extra to serve

2 eggs, separated

I cup sour cream

sunflower oil, for frying

2 bananas, sliced

**SERVES 4**

The bananas in these pancakes become caramelized in the hot skillet, and when you drizzle over some honey before serving, everything becomes even sweeter.

Preheat the oven to low.

Sift the flours, baking soda, and salt into a large mixing bowl. Put the honey, egg yolks, and sour cream in a bowl and beat to combine. Mix the wet ingredients with the dry ingredients until no lumps of flour remain.

Whisk the egg whites in a separate bowl with an electric handheld whisk until soft peaks form. Using a large metal spoon, fold the whites into the batter.

Heat a heavy-based skillet over medium heat. Grease the skillet with a kitchen towel dipped in oil. Drop 2–3 tablespoons of batter into the skillet. Cook for 1–2 minutes on the first side, until the edges look dry, then scatter over 3–4 slices of banana and flip the pancake over. Cook for 2 minutes, until golden and cooked through. Keep warm in the oven while you make the rest. Serve with honey, for drizzling.

# Dairy-free coconut pancakes with lime syrup & mango

I cup plus 2 tablespoons
all-purpose flour

3 teaspoons baking powder

¼ teaspoon salt

2 tablespoons brown sugar

3 tablespoons desiccated
coconut

¾ cup coconut milk

2 tablespoons sunflower
oil, plus extra for frying

I mango, peeled, pitted,
and sliced

**LIME SYRUP**

freshly squeezed juice
of 3 limes

grated zest of I lime

½ cup honey

6 cardamom pods, crushed

**SERVES 4**

These pancakes are completely dairy free; they don't even contain egg. This makes them a bit more dense but as they are drenched in a runny lime and honey syrup before serving, this is soon taken care of. Try to find the ripest, most perfumed mango to make this dish exquisite.

Preheat the oven to low.

To make the lime syrup, put the lime juice and zest, honey, and cardamom pods in a small saucepan and bring to a boil. Boil for 5 minutes, then remove from the heat and set aside.

Meanwhile, sift the flour, baking powder, and salt into a large mixing bowl and stir in the sugar and desiccated coconut. Put the coconut milk, ⅓ cup water, and the oil in a bowl and beat to

combine. Mix the wet ingredients with the dry ingredients until no lumps of flour remain.

Heat a heavy-based skillet over medium heat. Grease the skillet with a kitchen towel dipped in oil. Drop 2–3 tablespoons of batter into the skillet. Cook for 1–2 minutes on each side until golden and cooked through. Keep warm in the oven while you make the rest. Serve with mango and lime syrup.

*Dairy-free coconut pancakes with lime syrup & mango (left)*

# Buttermilk waffles with crème fraîche, bitter chocolate sauce, & hazelnuts

1 cup plus 2 tablespoons
  all-purpose flour

½ teaspoon baking soda

1 teaspoon baking powder

3 tablespoons sugar

2 eggs

1 teaspoon vanilla extract

3 tablespoons unsalted
  butter, melted, plus extra
  for cooking

1 generous cup buttermilk

3 tablespoons chopped
  hazelnuts

crème fraîche, to serve

**BITTER CHOCOLATE
  SAUCE**

3½ oz. bittersweet
  chocolate

1 tablespoon butter

*a waffle iron*

**SERVES 4**

*It is fairly indulgent to go for waffles with chocolate and crème fraîche before you have even ventured out into the world, but now and again, it's good to be decadent! The sauce is so easy and making it with water rather than cream is not a thrifty shortcut, but a way of bringing out the bitterness in the chocolate.*

Preheat the oven to low.

Sift the flour, baking soda, and baking powder into a large mixing bowl. Put the sugar, eggs, vanilla, butter, buttermilk, and ¼ cup water in a bowl and beat to combine. Pour the wet ingredients into the dry ingredients and whisk until blended. Don't worry about any small lumps. Set aside.

To make the bitter chocolate sauce, put the chocolate, butter, and ⅓ cup water in a heatproof bowl over a saucepan of gently simmering water. Do not let the base of the bowl touch the water. Let melt for 5 minutes. Remove from the heat and stir until smooth. Keep warm on the pan. Meanwhile, put the hazelnuts in a dry skillet over medium heat and let them heat up. Stir so they brown evenly, then remove from the heat.

When you're ready to cook the waffles, heat your waffle iron and grease with oil. Ladle in enough batter to fill it, then close. Check the manufacturer's instructions for cooking times, but it should need about 3–5 minutes. When ready, steam will stop escaping from the sides and the waffles will look crisp and golden. Keep warm in the oven while you cook the rest. Serve hot with crème fraîche, a drizzle of chocolate sauce, and a scattering of toasted hazelnuts.

# Gingerbread waffles with strawberries

1 cup plus 2 tablespoons
all-purpose flour
½ teaspoon baking soda
1 teaspoon baking powder
1 teaspoon ground
cinnamon
1 teaspoon ground ginger
⅛ teaspoon ground nutmeg
3 tablespoons molasses
2 eggs
3 tablespoons unsalted
butter, melted, plus extra
for cooking
¾ cup whole milk
honey and strawberries,
to serve
*a waffle iron*
**MAKES 8–12**

**Depending on the size and shape of your waffle iron, this recipe will make a batch of 8 or much more if your waffle maker makes thin ones. If you don't have such a contraption (not everyone feels the need for a waffle maker in their lives), you can make these into pancakes by simply cooking them in a heavy-based skillet or on a griddle.**

Preheat the oven to low.

Sift the flour, baking soda, baking powder, and spices in a large mixing bowl. Put the molasses, eggs, butter, and milk in a bowl and beat to combine. Pour the wet ingredients into the dry ingredients and beat to combine. Don't worry about any small lumps.

Heat your waffle iron and grease with oil. Ladle in enough batter to fill it, then close. Check the manufacturer's instructions for cooking times, but it should need about 3–5 minutes. When ready, steam will stop escaping from the sides and the waffles will look crisp and golden. Keep warm in the oven while you cook the rest. Serve hot with honey and a handful of the sweetest strawberries.

# entrées

Baked tomatoes stuffed with goat cheese & herbs  Pancetta, taleggio, roasted leek, & onion tart  **Cheesy polenta with sausages & red onions** English breakfast quiche  Zucchini fritters with tomato & feta salad **Garlic mushrooms & goat cheese on sourdough toast**  Corn cakes with bacon & avocado  Crab cakes with slaw & sweet chili sauce  **Hot smoked salmon hash with dill cream**  Sweet potato, chorizo, & fried egg hash Dukkah & harissa sausage rolls  **Smoked haddock kedgeree**  Linguine with lemon, basil, & parmesan cream

## Baked tomatoes stuffed with goat cheese & herbs

4 large, stuffing tomatoes
   such as Marmande or
   heirloom, or more of
   a smaller variety

2 tablespoons extra virgin
   olive oil, plus extra
   to drizzle

1 onion, finely chopped

1 tablespoon chopped
   fresh thyme leaves

6½ oz. goat cheese

¼ cup dried bread crumbs

2 eggs, beaten

a handful of fresh basil
   leaves

**SERVES 4**

Stuffed tomatoes are quite an old-fashioned idea, but I was reminded just how delectable they can be on a recent trip to France. When you see the quirky-looking shapes of the Marmande and heirloom tomatoes in their various shades of green and orange, that's the time to make this dish. The secret is to slightly undercook them so the tomatoes don't just collapse into amoeba-like blobs. I like to use quite a strong aged goat cheese for this, as it contrasts against the sweetness of the tomatoes when they are cooked.

Preheat the oven to 350°F.

Slice the top third off the tomatoes and reserve. Using a melon baller, scoop out the seeds and juices and discard or reserve for making a tomato sauce.

Heat the oil in a skillet, add the onion and thyme, and soften for 5 minutes. Let cool slightly.

Beat the goat cheese, bread crumbs, and eggs together and season well. Stir in the onion mixture and a few basil leaves. Spoon the stuffing into the tomatoes and top with the reserved hats. Arrange in a baking dish, drizzle with oil, and scatter over the remaining basil leaves. Bake in the preheated oven for 18–20 minutes.

# Pancetta, taleggio, roasted leek, & onion tart

2 leeks, sliced 1 in. thick

2 red onions, peeled and cut into slim wedges

2 tablespoons extra virgin olive oil, plus extra to drizzle

1 tablespoon balsamic vinegar

12 oz. puff pastry dough, thawed if frozen

5 oz. Taleggio (rind removed), cubed

8 wafer-thin slices of pancetta

2 handfuls of arugula

sea salt and freshly ground black pepper

**SERVES 4–6**

Roasted leeks are one of my favorite ways with vegetables. I love that they are sweet and crispy at the same time. They go brilliantly atop a tart, needing only creamy cheese to finish them off. I have used the soft, slightly stinky Taleggio in this version, but you could just as easily use a blue cheese or mozzarella.

Preheat the oven to 400°F.

Put the leeks, onions, oil, and balsamic vinegar in a roasting pan and season. Toss well, then roast in the preheated oven for 30–35 minutes, until soft. Leave the oven on for the tart.

Meanwhile, roll out the puff pastry dough into a rectangle, lay it on a baking sheet, and prick it all over with a fork.

When the roasting vegetables are soft and slightly charred, scatter them evenly over the pastry. Drop the cubed Taleggio all over, then drape the pancetta slices over everything. Bake in the oven for 25–30 minutes until the pastry is golden and well risen at the edges. Strew the arugula over the top and drizzle with a little extra olive oil before serving.

# Cheesy polenta with sausages & red onions

12 pork sausages

2 red onions, peeled and cut into slim wedges

a handful of fresh sage leaves

6 tablespoons olive oil

1 cup instant polenta

1 tablespoon chopped fresh thyme leaves

$1/2$ cup grated Parmesan

$1^{1}/_{3}$ cups crumbled feta

sea salt and freshly ground black pepper

*an 8-in. square pan, greased*

**SERVES 4**

If you are not yet sold on polenta, I urge you to try this method of preparation because it has converted many a person. The secret is that it needs to be seasoned well and enriched with lots of cheese, as well as being fried over high heat until golden so that you get the crunchy exterior and the soft creaminess inside.

Preheat the oven to 375°F.

Put the sausages and onions in a roasting pan. Scatter the sage over the top and drizzle with 2 tablespoons of the oil, then toss everything together. Roast in the preheated oven for 30–35 minutes, until golden and cooked through.

Bring $2^{2}/_{3}$ cups water to a boil with a pinch of salt and 1 tablespoon of the oil. Remove from the heat and pour in the polenta. Mix it with a wooden spoon and lots of elbow grease. Return to low heat

for about 2–3 minutes, stirring constantly. Remove from the heat, beat in the thyme and cheeses, and season generously. Spoon into the prepared pan and smooth out the surface. Let cool and set.

Tip the polenta onto a board and quarter, then cut each quarter in half to make triangles. Heat a skillet over high heat and add the remaining oil. Add as many polenta triangles as you can and fry for 2–3 minutes on each side, until golden. Serve with the sausage mixture.

*Cheesy polenta with sausages & red onions (left)*

# English breakfast quiche

Here are all the flavors of a traditional full farmhouse English fried breakfast in a quiche. Bake it the day before a long, early-morning journey when you have to have your breakfast on the go. Try to resist smothering it in ketchup!

**PASTRY DOUGH**

1¾ cups all-purpose flour

1 teaspoon English
mustard powder

10 tablespoons butter,
chilled and cubed

1 egg, beaten

**FILLING**

4 pork sausages

6½ oz. cherry tomatoes,
halved

6½ oz. thick-sliced bacon,
cut into matchsticks

6½ oz. button mushrooms,
halved

1 tablespoon olive oil

1¼ cups crème fraîche

3 extra-large eggs, beaten

1 teaspoon English
mustard powder

a 10-in. fluted, loose-
bottomed tart pan

baking beans

**SERVES 6**

Preheat the oven to 400°F.

To make the pastry dough, put the flour, mustard powder, and butter in a food processor and pulse until they are just combined. Add the egg and run the motor until the mixture just comes into a ball. Turn out, wrap with plastic wrap, and chill in the fridge for 30 minutes.

To make the filling, put the sausages in a roasting pan and roast in the preheated oven for 10 minutes. Take the pan out of the oven, throw in the tomatoes, bacon, and mushrooms, drizzle over the oil, and return to the oven to roast for 15–20 minutes, until everything is tender and cooked through. Leave the oven on.

Roll out the dough on a lightly floured surface until it is about ⅛ inch thick and use to line the tart pan. Press the dough into the corners and leave the overhang. Prick the base all over with a fork, line with parchment paper, and fill with baking beans. Bake in the oven for 8 minutes, then remove the beans and paper. Trim off the overhang and reduce the heat to 300°F. Return the crust to the oven for 2–3 minutes to dry out while you prepare the filling.

To finish the filling, slice the sausages and scatter them with the rest of the roasted ingredients into the crust. Mix the crème fraîche, eggs, and mustard powder and pour over everything in the crust. Bake for 30–35 minutes, until set around the edges. Turn off the oven and let the tart cool in the oven, with the door open, for 15 minutes. Cut into slices and serve warm or cold.

# Zucchini fritters with tomato & feta salad

3 zucchini, grated

1/2 red onion, finely chopped

1 teaspoon cumin seeds

2 red chiles, finely chopped

2/3 cup all-purpose flour

1/2 teaspoon baking soda

2 tablespoons fresh mint
leaves, chopped

2 eggs, beaten

1/4 cup olive oil

**TOMATO & FETA SALAD**

1 tablespoon red wine
vinegar

1/2 teaspoon English
mustard powder

3 tablespoons olive oil

3 tomatoes, chopped

4 scallions, sliced

1 1/3 cups crumbled feta

**SERVES 4**

These little fritters are a great way of using up zucchini if you have a glut of them in your garden. The zucchini are salted in order to remove some of the moisture (not the bitterness), otherwise they can be quite soggy. Seed the chiles for the fritters if you don't like the heat. You can serve the fritters with this tomato & feta salad or just a simple yogurt and mint dip, if you prefer.

Preheat the oven to low.

Put the zucchini and a good pinch of salt in a colander. Toss well to distribute the salt and leave for 20 minutes. Squeeze the zucchini to extract some of the moisture, then pat dry with paper towels.

Mix the zucchini with the onion, cumin seeds, chiles, flour, baking soda, mint, and eggs in a mixing bowl. The mixture will seem quite dry at first but the zucchini will moisten everything the more you stir. Season and leave for 10 minutes while you make the tomato & feta salad.

To make the tomato & feta salad, whisk together the vinegar and mustard powder, then add the oil and whisk until it emulsifies. Season. Put the tomatoes, scallions, feta, and dressing in a dish.

Heat the oil in a nonstick skillet over medium/high heat. Drop a heaping tablespoon of batter into the skillet. Cook in batches of 3–4 depending on the size of the skillet. Cook for 2–3 minutes on each side, until really golden and cooked through. Keep warm in the oven while you cook the rest. Serve with a mound of the tomato & feta salad.

# Garlic mushrooms & goat cheese on sourdough toast

8 brown mushrooms

3 garlic cloves, crushed

3 tablespoons olive oil

3 tablespoons pine nuts

2 tablespoons balsamic
vinegar

4 slices of sourdough
bread

5 oz. fresh goat cheese

fresh tarragon, to serve

sea salt and freshly ground
black pepper

**SERVES 4**

Garlicky mushrooms are great for breakfast, but try them on a layer of soft, creamy goat cheese and you will be in utter heaven. The kind of cheese you are looking for is a soft fresh cheese, not aged, so it will not have a rind. You could also use ricotta if you like. Seek out a good, sturdy rustic bread such as sourdough for this dish to prevent the underneath going soggy.

Preheat the oven to 400°F.

Put the mushrooms, garlic, and oil in a roasting pan. Toss well and season. Roast in the preheated oven for 15 minutes, until tender. Stir in the pine nuts and balsamic vinegar halfway through roasting.

Just before the mushrooms are ready, toast the slices of sourdough bread and spread with the goat cheese. Place the mushrooms on top, stalk side up, scatter with the tarragon, and serve immediately. Add more seasoning, if necessary.

*Garlic mushrooms & goat cheese on sourdough toast (left)*

# Corn cakes with bacon & avocado

2/3 cup self-rising flour

1/4 cup cornmeal

1/2 teaspoon baking soda

a pinch of cayenne pepper

2 extra-large eggs

2/3 cup sour cream

2 cups canned or frozen
   corn kernels

3 scallions, sliced

12 bacon slices

sunflower oil, for frying

1 avocado, pitted and sliced

a small handful of arugula

sea salt and freshly ground
   black pepper

**SERVES 4**

**If you are veering towards lunch rather than breakfast, you could serve this with a mound of baby spinach and arugula dressed in lemon and olive oil and perhaps a few roasted peppers strewn amongst the greens to make it more substantial.**

Preheat the broiler.

Put the flour, cornmeal, baking soda, and cayenne pepper in a mixing bowl. In a separate bowl, whisk together the eggs, sour cream, corn kernels, and scallions. Pour this into the dry ingredients, season, and mix until blended. The batter should be fairly firm.

Broil the bacon until really crisp.

Heat 2 tablespoons oil in a skillet over medium heat. Drop 2 tablespoons of batter into the skillet and cook in batches of about 3, depending on the size of the skillet. Cook the corn cakes for 2 minutes on each side, until golden brown and cooked through. Transfer to a plate and cover with foil to keep warm while you cook the rest.

Serve the corn cakes with a few slices of avocado, the crisp bacon, and a couple of arugula leaves. Grind over some black pepper.

# Crab cakes with slaw & sweet chili sauce

1 lb. lump crabmeat

1/2 cup dried bread crumbs

1 egg, beaten

3 tablespoons mayonnaise

a pinch of cayenne pepper

3 tablespoons chopped
   cilantro leaves

1/4 cup olive oil

sea salt and freshly ground
   black pepper

sweet chili sauce, to serve

**SLAW**

1 apple, peeled

2 carrots

1/2 small red cabbage

6 scallions, sliced

freshly squeezed juice
   of 1 lime

1/4 cup mayonnaise

1 garlic clove, crushed

**SERVES 4**

**Crab cakes are not cheap to make so it's a good choice when you have people coming over for more of a fancy lunchy brunch.**

Put the crabmeat, bread crumbs, egg, mayonnaise, cayenne pepper, and cilantro in a large mixing bowl, season, and mix until blended. Shape the mixture into 8 x 3-inch patties and lay on a sheet of parchment paper on a baking sheet. Chill in the refrigerator for 1 hour.

Preheat the oven to low.

To make the slaw, feed the apple and carrots through the grater on your food processor, or do it by hand if you don't have one. Shred the cabbage by hand as thinly as you can, or use the slicing attachment on the food processor. Tip everything into a large bowl. Add the scallions, lime juice, mayonnaise, and garlic and stir well. Set aside while you finish the crab cakes.

Heat the oil in a large skillet over high heat. Fry the crab cakes in batches (keeping them warm in the oven as you go) for 3–4 minutes on each side, until crisp and deep golden.

Spoon a mound of slaw onto each plate and serve 2 crab cakes on top. Serve with sweet chili sauce.

*Corn cakes with bacon & avocado (right)*

# Hot smoked salmon hash with dill cream

1 lb. new potatoes, halved

¼ cup olive oil

2 onions, sliced

5 oz. bacon, chopped

1 tablespoon butter

2 teaspoons capers

6½ oz. hot smoked salmon,
broken into large chunks

⅔ cup crème fraîche

freshly squeezed juice and
grated zest of 1 lime

1 tablespoon chopped
fresh dill

sea salt and freshly ground
black pepper

**SERVES 4**

Unlike the regular smoked salmon we know so well, hot smoked salmon looks cooked and flakes into beautiful chunks. Mixing it with bacon works really well as they share the same smokiness. A dollop of crème fraîche infused with lime and dill adds a bit of well-needed freshness too.

Put a saucepan of water over medium heat and bring to a boil. Add a pinch of salt and the potatoes. Reduce the heat and let it simmer for 12–15 minutes, until the potatoes are tender.

Meanwhile, put half the oil, the onions, and bacon in a skillet. Cover with a lid and cook over low heat for 8–10 minutes, stirring occasionally, until softening. Remove the lid, turn up the heat slightly, and cook for 3–4 minutes until slightly golden. Tip onto a plate and set aside.

Drain the potatoes and add the butter and remaining oil to the skillet you just used for the onion mixture. Add the potatoes and cook over high heat for 5–6 minutes, until browning on all sides. Stir in the onion mixture, capers, and salmon and cook for 3–4 minutes, until everything is sizzling and hot, then season.

Mix the crème fraîche, lime zest, and enough juice to make it limey but not too runny. Stir in the dill and season. Serve the hash with a dollop of the dill cream.

# Sweet potato, chorizo, & fried egg hash

3 sweet potatoes,
peeled and cubed

2 red onions, peeled and
cut into wedges

1 red chile, sliced

1 teaspoon cumin seeds

¼ cup extra virgin olive oil

5 oz. chorizo, sliced

6½ oz. cherry tomatoes,
halved

4 eggs

a handful of fresh flatleaf
parsley leaves, chopped

sea salt and freshly ground
black pepper

**SERVES 4**

This is full of sweet, smoky flavors. I adore vibrant orange sweet potatoes for their unusual starchy taste and I find that anything containing chorizo quickly becomes a firm favorite in our home. Add a fried egg and you can't go wrong!

Preheat the oven to 350°F.

Put the potatoes, onions, chile, cumin seeds, and half the oil in a roasting pan and toss well. Roast in the preheated oven for 15 minutes. Remove the pan from the oven, throw in the chorizo and tomatoes, and return to the oven for 20 minutes, until everything is tender and slightly charred.

Heat the remaining oil in a skillet over high heat, then crack an egg in each corner and turn the heat right down. Cook for 2–3 minutes until the white has set. If you need to firm up the white, cover with the lid for 30 seconds.

Season the hash and stir in the parsley. Serve each portion of hash with a fried egg on top.

*Hot smoked salmon hash with dill cream (left)*

# Dukkah & harissa sausage rolls

1 lb. ground lamb

1 teaspoon smoked
  paprika

1 teaspoon ground
  cinnamon

¼ cup harissa or sun-dried
  tomato paste

1 lb. puff pastry dough,
  thawed if frozen

1 egg, beaten

sea salt and freshly ground
  black pepper

**DUKKAH**

2 tablespoons sesame
  seeds

2 tablespoons pine nuts

1 teaspoon coriander
  seeds

1 teaspoon cumin seeds

*a baking sheet, lightly oiled*

**SERVES 4**

The plain old sausage roll gets a bit of an exotic makeover here. When I realized that most people like to drench their sausage rolls in tomato ketchup I thought, why not add some tomato to the meat. Hopefully this is enough to prevent my rolls from the ketchup fate. Not only have I used lamb, not pork, for the filling, but I have also spiced it with cinnamon and smoked paprika. And the top is speckled with an Egyptian spice blend called dukkah. This blend varies from recipe to recipe, so feel free to use up any remnants of nuts or seeds that you have.

Preheat the oven to 400°F.

To make the dukkah, put the sesame seeds, pine nuts, coriander seeds, cumin seeds, and a pinch of salt in a mortar. Bash them with the pestle until crushed, but try to maintain a little texture so they are not pounded into a powder.

Put the lamb, paprika, cinnamon, and harissa in a mixing bowl with some seasoning and mix with your hands, squelching it all together until thoroughly blended together.

Roll out the pastry on a lightly floured work surface until you have a rectangle 10 x 24 inches (and about ⅛ inch thick). Cut into 4, at 6-inch intervals. This will give you 4 rectangles, each 10 x 6 inches. Spoon about 4 tablespoons of the sausage mixture onto each rectangle. Brush a little beaten egg along one short side. Fold the pastry over from one short side to meet the other short side. Press the folded edges together to seal and crimp by pressing down with a fork. Leave the other 2 sides of the rolls open so that you can still see the filling.

Repeat to make 3 more rolls. Brush them with more beaten egg and sprinkle the dukkah over the top. Transfer to the prepared baking sheet and bake in the preheated oven for 25–35 minutes, until golden and cooked through.

# Smoked haddock kedgeree

3 tablespoons butter

2 onions, thinly sliced

4 eggs

1 teaspoon ground cumin

1 teaspoon ground
coriander

$\frac{1}{2}$ teaspoon ground
turmeric

$\frac{3}{4}$ cup plus 2 tablespoons
basmati rice

1$\frac{1}{4}$ cups boiling water

14 oz. smoked haddock

freshly squeezed juice
of 1 lemon

a handful of fresh curly
parsley leaves, chopped

**SERVES 4**

Kedgeree is an old English dish left over from the Victorian days when, in a flurry of Anglo-Indian mania, it graced breakfast tables around the land. It developed from a simple Indian dish of rice and lentils called khichari.

Bring a small saucepan of water to a boil for the eggs. Meanwhile, melt the butter in a casserole dish over low heat, add the onions, and stir to coat in the butter. Cook, covered, for 10 minutes, stirring occasionally, until soft. Put the eggs in the pan of boiling water and turn it down to a gentle simmer. Simmer for 8 minutes. Drain and run them under cold water. Take the lid off the onions, add the spices, and turn up the heat. Cook, stirring, for 3–4 minutes, until the onions are golden brown. Add the rice, stir, and pour in the 1$\frac{1}{4}$ cups boiling water. Cover with the lid and turn the heat down so it gently simmers for 8 minutes.

Put the haddock in a skillet and cover with boiling water. Simmer gently for 5–6 minutes, until cooked though, then drain. Turn off the heat under the rice, keep covered, and let steam for 10 minutes. Peel and halve the eggs. Drain the fish and remove the skin and any bones. Flake into chunks and stir into the rice with the lemon juice and parsley. Serve topped with the boiled eggs.

# Linguine with lemon, basil, & parmesan cream

2 tablespoons butter

2 shallots, finely chopped

1 unwaxed lemon

1$\frac{1}{4}$ cups whipping cream

$\frac{3}{4}$ hot chicken or
vegetable stock

2 handfuls of fresh basil
leaves, plus more to
serve

12 oz. dried linguine

2$\frac{1}{2}$ oz. Parmesan or
Pecorino shavings,
plus extra to serve

sea salt and freshly ground
black pepper

**SERVES 4**

I'm not suggesting you have pasta for breakfast, but if your brunch is a late one, this is an easy dish to whip up. I sometimes add a splash of vodka to the shallots too, which just gives it a slight acidic edge, as wine does. Make sure you go for unwaxed lemons so you are not ingesting all the horrid chemicals on waxed ones.

Heat the butter in a skillet and add the shallots. Add a pinch of salt, cover, and cook over low heat for 6–7 minutes, stirring every now and then, until soft and glossy.

Put a large saucepan of water on to boil for the pasta. Meanwhile, take a potato peeler and pare off the zest of the lemon, leaving behind the white pith. Try to pare the zest in one long piece so you can easily remove it later.

Add the cream, stock, lemon zest, and basil to the shallots and gently simmer for 10–15 minutes, uncovered, until it has reduced and thickened—it should only just coat the back of a spoon. Cook the linguine in the boiling water until al dente.

Season the sauce with a little salt and lots of pepper. Fish out the lemon zest. Drain the pasta and return to the pan. Stir in the Parmesan and squeeze in some juice from the lemon. Add more juice or seasoning, to taste. Garnish with more basil and Parmesan shavings.

*Linguine with lemon, basil, & parmesan cream (left)*

# sandwiches, salads, & sides

Steak & fried egg sandwiches with mustard butter  Hot chorizo, avocado, & lime sandwiches  **Gravadlax with pickles on rye bread** Reubens sandwiches with horseradish sauce  Spiced omelet sandwiches with tomato & chile jam  **Quinoa salad with smoked chicken, avocado, pea shoots, & toasted almonds**  Red rice, dried cherry, & pistachio salad with halloumi  Pickled herring, beet, fennel, & belgian endive salad with yogurt dressing  **Hash browns**  Bacon & onion rösti  Baked beans with maple syrup & paprika  **Bacon rolls with chile & pecans**  Roasted balsamic tomatoes

# Steak & fried egg sandwiches with mustard butter

7 tablespoons butter, softened

2 teaspoons whole-grain mustard

½ teaspoon English mustard powder

1 tablespoon chopped fresh tarragon leaves

1 teaspoon Gentleman's relish or anchovy paste (optional)

2 white bakery buns, halved horizontally

2 x 8-oz. rib-eye or sirloin steaks, roughly ⅝ inch thick

3 tablespoons olive oil

2 extra-large eggs

sea salt and freshly ground black pepper

**SERVES 2**

A well-cooked steak with a rosy interior and charred exterior truly is a wonderful thing. I like to adorn it with a butter spiked with the piquant flavor of mustard and tarragon. When the steak is ready, it is clamped in a soft white bun slathered in this delicious butter, which will melt with the steak's residual heat. Along with a fried egg cooked so it is only just runny inside, this is one sandwich that you need to eat fast before the egg and butter have time to trickle down your chin.

Put the butter in a mixing bowl and beat it with a spoon until squished against the sides of the bowl. Spoon in the whole-grain mustard, mustard powder, tarragon, and Gentleman's relish, if using. Season to taste, taking care not to overseason as the relish will already be salty. Beat everything together and use to butter the insides of the buns.

Heat a ridged stovetop grill pan over high heat until very hot. Brush the steaks with 1 tablespoon of the oil and season. Using tongs, lay the steaks on the pan and press down. Let them cook for 2–4 minutes on each side. Press on the center of the steak to determine how well cooked it is. A light yield means it is medium, while anything soft is still rare. Transfer the steaks to a board and cut off any large pieces of fat. Let rest for 2–3 minutes while you cook the eggs.

Add the remaining oil to a skillet and heat over high heat. Crack in the eggs and turn the heat to low. Cook for 2 minutes, then flip over for 30 seconds to cook the other side, but leave the yolk with a bit of ooze. Place a steak in each bun and finish off with a fried egg.

# Hot chorizo, avocado, & lime sandwiches

1 avocado

freshly squeezed juice of ½ lime

4 oz. chorizo, sliced diagonally

4 slices of country-style bread

a handful of arugula

sea salt and freshly ground black pepper

**SERVES 2**

A good nutty avocado is hard to beat. All it needs is some lime juice to perk up the natural flavors. Pair it with sweet, spicy chorizo and you instantly have the perfect sandwich.

Halve the avocado and remove the pit. Using a spoon, scoop out the flesh and mash in a bowl with the lime juice and some seasoning. Set aside.

Heat a skillet over high heat, then add the chorizo. Fry for 1 minute on each side, or until crisp and lightly browned. Remove from the heat.

Toast the bread and spread the avocado over 2 slices. Top with the chorizo and a handful of arugula and sandwich with the other piece of toast.

*Steak & fried egg sandwiches with mustard butter (right)*

# Gravadlax with pickles on rye bread

buttered dark rye bread,
to serve

**GRAVADLAX**

1 tablespoon juniper
berries

1 tablespoon fennel seeds

1 tablespoon black
peppercorns

¼ cup coarse sea salt

¼ cup demerara sugar

1½ lbs. salmon fillet, about
1 inch thick, pin boned
and scaled

**PICKLES**

2 cucumbers, sliced
¼ in. thick

1 small onion, thinly sliced

2 tablespoons sea salt

¼ teaspoon celery seeds

1 teaspoon mustard seeds

2 tablespoons prepared
horseradish

5 whole cloves

1 cup white wine vinegar

1 cup sugar

**SERVES 6–8**

I like to make this for a brunch party as it feeds many unexpected guests without any extra effort. Making both the pickles and gravadlax is mainly an assault on your spice cabinet, so don't be put off by the long list of ingredients. Refrigerated pickles will keep for up to 1 month, which is why the recipe makes a lot more than you can eat in one sitting. The gravadlax is very easy although it does need to be thought about a few days earlier, but once it is done you can forget about it. Make sure you start with the freshest fish as it is ultimately eaten cured but raw.

To make the pickles, put the cucumbers, onion, and salt in a large nonmetal bowl. Cover and chill in the refrigerator for 2 hours. Rinse and drain well. Transfer to a medium container. In a small saucepan, heat the celery seeds, mustard seeds, horseradish, cloves, vinegar, and sugar. Bring to a boil, to dissolve the sugar, then pour onto the container with the cucumbers. Cover and refrigerate for 1 day to develop a full flavor.

To make the gravadlax, pound the juniper berries, fennel seeds, peppercorns, 1 tablespoon of the salt, and the sugar with a pestle and mortar until roughly crushed and aromatic.

Line a nonmetal tray with plastic wrap, leaving enough overlapping to wrap around the salmon later. Scatter one-quarter of the ground spices over the plastic wrap and lay the salmon, skin side down, on top. Cover with the rest of the ground spices. Wrap tightly in the plastic wrap so you form a watertight parcel and weight down with cans of food or a heavy board. Let cure for 12 hours or overnight in the fridge. Flip the fish over, weight down again, and cure for another 12 hours and continue to cure and flip until the fish has had 48 hours.

Unwrap the fish and drain off any juices. Place on a board, skin side down. Slice the gravadlax thinly with a sharp knife, cutting the flesh away from the skin (discard the skin). Serve with buttered rye bread and pickles.

# Reubens sandwiches with horseradish sauce

¼ cup mayonnaise

3 scallions, sliced

2 gherkins, chopped

¼ teaspoon hot
horseradish sauce

a dash of Worcestershire
sauce

a pinch of sugar

8 slices of rye bread

10 oz. corned or salt beef,
sliced

I cup sauerkraut, drained

3½ oz. sliced Emmenthal

**SERVES 4**

**This is a classic sandwich which contains corned beef (or salt beef), Thousand Island Dressing, sauerkraut, and melted Swiss cheese. I am not a huge fan of the dressing so I have tweaked mine slightly.**

Put the mayonnaise, scallions, gherkins, horseradish and Worcestershire sauces, and sugar in a bowl, mix well, and set aside.

Preheat the broiler.

Toast the bread under the broiler for 1–2 minutes on one side, until golden. Remove from the oven and spread dressing over the untoasted side of half the slices. Lay the Emmenthal on the rest and broil for 2–3 minutes to melt.

Meanwhile, put the corned beef, then some sauerkraut over the mayonnaise-covered bread slices. Once the cheese has melted, make up the sandwiches and serve immediately.

# Spiced omelet sandwiches with tomato & chile jam

8 extra-large eggs

I teaspoon ground cumin

a small handful of cilantro
leaves, chopped

2 tablespoons olive oil

I long baguette

2½ oz. lamb's lettuce

sea salt and freshly ground
black pepper

**TOMATO & CHILE JAM**

8 oz. tomatoes, chopped

2 large red chiles, seeded
and chopped, plus I just
chopped

I red onion, chopped

3 garlic cloves, sliced

½ in. fresh ginger, grated

¼ cup red wine vinegar

1¼ cups demerara sugar

2 tablespoons fish sauce

**SERVES 4**

**The tomato & chile jam for these sandwiches is made in the oven. Watch it doesn't get too sticky as it will set and harden more on cooling, a bit like jam does. It makes a jarful but you can use it up on other dishes, as it will keep for a month in the fridge. I like using the extra with grilled fish and a dollop of sour cream.**

Preheat the oven to 400°F.

To make the tomato & chile jam, put the tomatoes, chiles, onion, garlic, ginger, vinegar, and sugar in a roasting pan. Season with fish sauce, stir to combine, and roast in the preheated oven for 30–40 minutes, until the tomatoes and onion are well cooked and caramelized. The jam will still be runny but will thicken as it cools. Let cool slightly.

Beat together the eggs, cumin, and cilantro and season. Heat a skillet (about 8 inches in diameter), add the oil, and swirl to coat the base of the skillet.

Pour in half the egg mixture and draw the cooked edges into the center. Tilt the skillet so the uncooked egg runs into the edges. When the omelet is evenly set except for a little unset egg, it is done. Fold it in half and slide it out of the skillet onto a board. Cook the remaining egg mixture in the same way.

Slice the baguette horizontally. Slice each omelet in half and stuff into the baguette. Smear with tomato & chile jam (lots if everyone likes the heat) and add a tangle of lamb's lettuce. Cut the baguette into 4 portions and serve.

*Reubens sandwiches with horseradish sauce (right)*

# Quinoa salad with smoked chicken, avocado, pea shoots, & toasted almonds

1²⁄₃ cups quinoa

½ cup shelled Marcona almonds, chopped

⅓ cup extra virgin olive oil

3 tablespoons sherry vinegar

1 garlic clove, crushed

10 oz. smoked chicken, chopped

2 avocados, pitted and chopped

1 cup cherry tomatoes, halved

a handful of pea shoots

sea salt and freshly ground black pepper

**SERVES 4**

Quinoa is a grain with a very high protein content. It has a slightly frog spawn look about it, but it tastes like a nutty couscous or bulgur wheat. I adore pea shoots, which seem to be the ingredient *de rigueur*; they taste of peas but have the texture of a soft leaf. Along with smoky chicken and creamy avocado this makes a really gorgeous warm salad for a sunny mid-morning.

Soak the quinoa in a bowl of cold water for 20 minutes.

Meanwhile, put the almonds in a dry skillet over medium heat and let them heat up. Stir so they brown evenly, then remove from the heat.

Bring a pan of 2½ cups water to a boil and when the quinoa has had its time, drain and pour into the boiling water. Cook for 15 minutes.

Make a dressing by whisking together the oil, vinegar, garlic, and some seasoning.

Put the chicken, avocados, tomatoes, and toasted almonds in a large serving dish. When the quinoa is ready, drain it well and run it under cold water to stop it cooking. Drain again and tip into the dish with the vegetables. Add the dressing and toss together until blended. Gently fold in the pea shoots and serve.

# Red rice, dried cherry, & pistachio salad with halloumi

1¼ cups Camargue red rice

⅔ cup dried sour cherries

¼ cup extra virgin olive oil

1 tablespoon red wine vinegar

1 garlic clove, crushed

⅓ cup shelled pistachios

6 scallions, sliced

8 oz. halloumi, sliced

2 tablespoons chopped fresh mint leaves

¼ cup chopped fresh flatleaf parsley leaves

sea salt and freshly ground black pepper

**SERVES 4**

The red rice from the Camargue region of France has a nutty texture. It needs a punchy dressing to wake it up so I have added a crushed garlic clove to a regular vinaigrette. Look out for dried sour cherries for this vibrant salad, but you can use dried cranberries or raisins as a fallback.

Bring a medium saucepan of water to a boil and add the rice. Add a pinch of salt and simmer for 25–30 minutes, until the rice is tender but still has a bite to it.

Meanwhile, soak the cherries in ½ cup warm water, until they become really plump.

Make a dressing by whisking together 3 tablespoons of the oil, the vinegar, and garlic, and some seasoning. Drain the cherries and put in a large serving dish

with the pistachios and scallions.

Heat a ridged stovetop grill pan over high heat. Brush the halloumi with the remaining oil and grill for 1–2 minutes on each side, until branded with deep golden lines.

Drain the rice very well and add to the ingredients in the serving dish. Add the dressing and herbs and toss everything together until blended. Spoon onto plates and top with the halloumi.

## Pickled herring, beet, fennel, & belgian endive salad with yogurt dressing

3–4 tablespoons olive oil

freshly squeezed juice
of 1 lemon

1 fennel, trimmed and
thinly sliced

sprig of fresh dill, chopped

8 oz. cooked or raw
baby beets

½ cup Greek yogurt

1 tablespoon red wine
vinegar

2 heads of Belgian endive,
sliced

9 oz. pickled herring, cubed

sea salt and freshly ground
black pepper

**SERVES 4**

**Pickled herring, or rollmops as they are sometimes known, are great in the morning as they are zingy and sweet. Mixed with slivers of fennel and a few bitter endive leaves, they make for a very refined salad.**

Mix together 3 tablespoons of the oil and the lemon juice, then put half of it into a large mixing bowl with the fennel and dill. Season well, toss together, and set aside for 1 hour to soften the fennel. If you need to cook your beets, preheat the oven to 400°F.

To cook the beets, scrub, then put in a small roasting pan with the remaining oil and some seasoning. Cover with aluminum foil and roast in the preheated oven for 25–30 minutes, until tender. Cut this, or your precooked beets, into quarters.

Stir the yogurt and vinegar into the remaining oil and lemon juice dressing until well blended. Season to taste.

Add the endive to the fennel in the bowl. Top with the beets and herring and serve with the yogurt dressing.

# Hash browns

These hash browns are deep fried, which means you probably won't be making them every day, but like fries, it's great to sometimes make your own. If you need to keep them warm while you cook the rest of your breakfast, put them in the oven but lay them on a wire rack first so they don't go soggy.

2 tablespoons butter
1 onion, chopped
1¼ lbs. large potatoes,
    peeled and grated
1 egg white, beaten
vegetable oil,
    for deep-frying
sea salt and freshly ground
    black pepper
**MAKES 16**

Heat the butter in a skillet, then add the onion, cover with a lid, and cook over low heat until soft.

Put the potatoes into a large mixing bowl and stir in the softened onions. Stir in the egg white and season generously.

Fill a large saucepan one-third full with vegetable oil. Heat to 375°F (or until a blob of the potato mixture browns within a few seconds).

Roll the potato mixture into walnut-size balls, then flatten slightly before adding to the hot oil. Fry in batches of 4–5 for 2–3 minutes, until golden brown. Drain on paper towels and serve with extra salt, for sprinkling.

# Bacon & onion rösti

2 tablespoons unsalted
butter
1 onion, sliced
2½ oz. thick-sliced bacon,
cut into matchsticks
2 tablespoons chopped
fresh sage leaves
1½ lbs. Yukon gold
potatoes, peeled
and grated
sea salt and freshly ground
black pepper
*an 8-inch nonstick skillet*

**SERVES 4**

**There is something very comforting about lovely crispy rösti. It makes a good side dish to broiled sausages too.**

Melt half the butter in the skillet over low heat. Add the onion and bacon, raise the heat to medium, and cook for 7–8 minutes, until soft and lightly browned. Stir in the sage, then tip into a mixing bowl with the potatoes.

Add the remaining butter to the skillet. When it stops foaming, spread the potato mixture over the base of the skillet and press down well with the back of a spoon. Fry for 6–7 minutes without moving it. When it's golden underneath, flip it over and cook for the same amount on the other side too. Serve cut into wedges.

## Baked beans with maple syrup & paprika

2 x 14-oz. cans soldier, white navy, or pinto beans, or 14 oz. dried beans

2 tablespoons butter

8 oz. bacon or pancetta

2 onions, chopped

1 teaspoon Spanish smoked paprika

2 teaspoons Dijon mustard

1 tablespoon tomato paste

1 cup hot stock

⅓ cup pure maple syrup

sea salt and freshly ground black pepper

**SERVES 4**

**These homemade baked beans are utterly delicious. They are sweet and smoky and so irresistible. I like them piled on toasted and buttered whole-grain bread, or served with some hash browns if I am feeling really naughty.**

If using dried beans, put them in large bowl. Add enough water to cover by 3 inches and let stand overnight. The next day, drain the beans and put them in a saucepan of water. Bring to a boil and simmer for 40 minutes until tender. Drain.

Preheat the oven to 300°F.

Heat the butter in a large ovenproof casserole dish and fry the bacon until it has browned. Add the onions, paprika, and mustard. Reduce the heat to low, cover with a lid, and cook for 5 minutes,

stirring occasionally, until it smells utterly irresistible.

Add the cooked or canned beans, tomato paste, stock, and some seasoning. Cover with a lid and bake in the preheated oven for 2 hours.

Give everything a good stir, add the maple syrup, and taste to check the seasoning. Bake for a further 20 minutes with the lid off until the sauce has thickened. Serve with hot buttered toast or Hash Browns (see page 126).

# Bacon rolls with chile & pecans

¼–½ teaspoon ground
    red chile
2 tablespoons demerara
    sugar
3 tablespoons shelled
    pecans
8 oz. bacon slices
**MAKES 16**

**These little rolls make a great change to regular crispy fried bacon. They are sweet but also have a fiery kick and a crisp texture from the chopped nuts.**

Preheat the oven to 400°F.

Put the ground red chile, sugar, and pecans in a food processor and briefly blend until chopped but still coarse. Lay the slices of bacon on a baking sheet and scatter a little of the ground mixture over them. Roll up each slice and scatter a little more of the ground mixture over the top of each roll. Bake in the preheated oven for 15 minutes, until crisp.

# Roasted balsamic tomatoes

6 plum tomatoes
2 teaspoons sugar
sprig of fresh thyme,
    leaves only
2 tablespoons olive oil
2 tablespoons balsamic
    vinegar
sea salt and freshly ground
    black pepper
**SERVES 4**

**Roasted tomatoes make a lovely change from fried tomatoes. They go really well with Hash Browns (see page 126) or the Bacon Rolls above, but you could just as easily eat them cold in salads.**

Preheat the oven to 300°F.

Slice the plum tomatoes in half lengthwise and arrange, cut side up, on a baking sheet. Scatter over the sugar, thyme, oil, and vinegar and season.

Roast in the preheated oven for 1 hour, until they have lost some of their juiciness. Turn off the oven. Let them cool in the oven if there is time (to concentrate the flavors even further) or serve hot.

*Bacon rolls with chile & pecans, and Roasted balsamic tomatoes (left)*

# preserves

Peanut butter  Plum kernel jam  **Rhubarb & ginger jam**  Passion fruit curd  Grapefruit & cardamom marmalade  **Strawberry jam**  White chocolate praline spread

# Peanut butter

2 cups shelled raw peanuts

2 teaspoons sea salt

5 tablespoons groundnut oil

2 tablespoons honey

*a large baking sheet with sides*

*2 x half-pint preserving jars, sterilized (see page 4), with screw bands and new lids*

**MAKES ABOUT 2 X HALF-PINT JARS**

**Why I've never thought about making my own peanut butter mystifies me. It is so easy and so much better than the storebought variety. You can make it with cashews and almonds too, which would make fabulous gifts.**

Preheat the oven to 350°F.

Put the peanuts, salt, and 1 tablespoon of the oil in a large freezer bag and seal. Toss until the nuts are well coated. Tip out onto a large baking sheet with sides, making sure the nuts are in a single layer. Roast in the preheated oven for 6–8 minutes, until lightly golden. Stir halfway through. Remove from the oven and let cool.

Put the nuts in a food processor and blend until roughly chopped. Remove a third of the nuts now if you want crunchy peanut butter. Add the honey to the remaining paste, scrape down the edges of the bowl, and blend again. Trickle in the remaining oil and keep blending until you have a very smooth, spreadable paste. Fold in the chopped nuts. Transfer to the sterilized jars and use within 3 weeks.

# Plum kernel jam

1½ cups (about 11) plums, halved

3¾ cups sugar

1¼ cups boiling water

freshly squeezed juice of ½ lemon

*5 x half-pint preserving jars, sterilized (see page 4), with screw bands and new lids*

**MAKES ABOUT 5 X HALF-PINT JARS**

**The kernels hidden inside plum pits give off an ambrosial aroma. I am lucky enough to have a plum tree in my garden so I have become very adept at this jam.**

Remove the pits from the plums. Put the pits in a freezer bag and whack with a rolling pin until they break and release the kernel. You only need 6 kernels, so discard the rest. Put the plum halves and sugar in a large, nonmetal bowl, cover, and leave overnight.

The next day, put 2 or 3 saucers in the refrigerator. Put the reserved plum kernels in a wide saucepan with the boiling water and lemon juice and bring back to a boil. Add the plums and sugar and cook for 20 minutes, or until they collapse. Squash them with the back of a spoon to help break up any large pieces, if necessary.

Raise the heat and boil for about 20–25 minutes, or until the gelling point has been reached—a candy thermometer should read 220°F. To perform the gel test, put ½ teaspoon of the jam on a chilled saucer, return it to the refrigerator or freezer for about 30 seconds or until cold, then prod the top. If a skin has formed, the jam is ready. If not, return to the heat to cook for a little longer and retest it.

Ladle the hot jam into the sterilized jars, filling to within ¼ inch from the top. Wipe rims with a clean, damp cloth. Seal jars with lids and screw bands. Label with the date and store in a cool, dark place for up to 6 months.

*Peanut butter and Plum kernel jam (right)*

# Rhubarb & ginger jam

Rhubarb has that unique slightly metallic tang to it that you either love or loathe. I happen to love it and adore jam made from it. Ginger and rhubarb have a natural affinity, but the vanilla helps to soften the flavors.

2 lbs. rhubarb, trimmed

4 cups sugar

freshly squeezed juice
  of 2 lemons

2 in. fresh ginger, bruised

1 vanilla bean, halved
  lengthwise

4 x half-pint preserving
  jars, sterilized (see
  page 4), with screw
  bands and new lids

**MAKES ABOUT 4 X HALF-
PINT JARS**

Chop the rhubarb into 2-inch lengths and drop into a nonmetal bowl with the sugar. Cover and leave overnight.

The next day, put 2 or 3 saucers in the refrigerator.

Transfer the rhubarb mixture to a wide saucepan with the lemon juice and ginger. Scrape the seeds out of the vanilla bean and add to the pan along with the scraped bean. Bring to a boil, then cook over low heat until the sugar has dissolved.

Raise the heat and boil for about 15–30 minutes—the timing will depend on whether you are using delicate forced rhubarb or tougher green rhubarb—or until the gelling point has been reached. A candy thermometer should read 220°F. To perform the gel test, put $\frac{1}{2}$ teaspoon of the jam on a chilled saucer, return it to the refrigerator or freezer for about 30 seconds or until cold, then prod the top. If a skin has formed, the jam is ready. If not, return to the heat to cook for a little longer and retest it.

Fish out the ginger and vanilla bean and discard. Ladle the hot jam into the sterilized jars, filling to within $\frac{1}{4}$ inch from the top. Wipe rims with a clean, damp cloth. Seal jars with lids and screw bands. Label with the date and store in a cool, dark place for up to 6 months.

# Passion fruit curd

**If you're a fan of lemon curd, then you will love this. It is a little more perfumed than its lemony relative and somewhat sweeter. It goes brilliantly on any kind of bread or sandwiched between little meringues as a teatime treat.**

⅔ cup passion fruit pulp
(from about 6 fruit)
freshly squeezed juice
of 1 lemon
3 whole eggs
3 egg yolks
½ cup sugar
7 tablespoons unsalted
butter, chilled and cubed
2 x half-pint preserving jars,
sterilized (see page 4),
with screw bands and
new lids
**MAKES ABOUT 2 X HALF-
PINT JARS**

Bring a saucepan of water to a boil.

Take a heatproof bowl that will sit over your pan of boiling water. Sieve the passion fruit pulp into the bowl and add the lemon juice, all the eggs, and the sugar. Whisk until well mixed and set the bowl over the top of the pan of boiling water. Reduce the heat to low. Continue to whisk the mixture every 30 seconds,

until it thickens. This should take about 10–15 minutes. Turn the heat off and add the cubed butter, whisking it in until the curd thickens.

Remove from the heat and continue to whisk until the mixture has cooled down. Transfer to the sterilized jars. Label with the date and keep refrigerated for up to 2 weeks.

# Grapefruit & cardamom marmalade

2 grapefruits

4 lemons

about 4½ cups sugar,
or more

12 cardamom pods,
crushed and seeds
reserved

*12-in. square of cheesecloth*

*6 x half-pint preserving jars,
sterilized (see page 4),
with screw bands and
new lids*

**MAKES ABOUT 6 X HALF-
PINT JARS**

**This is a very practical, easy way of making marmalade. The nonsense with cheesecloth jelly bags is simplified to make your life easier. The only thing you want to remember is you need to start the process a day early to give it time to extract the pectin. I love the tang of cardamom, which adds an unexpected level of flavor, but leave it out if you prefer.**

Wash the grapefruits. Finely grate the zest, then wrap it up well with plastic wrap and set aside until you need it the next day.

Halve the lemons and squeeze the juice into a large nonmetal bowl, adding the pips. Halve the naked grapefruits and squeeze the juice into the bowl (discard the pips). Chop up the lemon and grapefruit shells and add to the bowl with 2 quarts water. Cover with a clean kitchen towel and leave in a cool place overnight.

The next day, put 2 or 3 saucers in the refrigerator. Put the contents of the bowl into a large preserving pan or nonaluminum saucepan and bring to a boil over medium heat. Cover with a lid, then simmer for about 1 hour.

Remove from the heat and let cool slightly. Line a strainer with your square of cheesecloth and set the strainer over a large bowl. Pour the mixture through to strain out the solids. Press down on the cooked fruit shells to extract as much

juice as possible, then discard them. Measure the juice (you should have about 5 cups), then weigh out the correct amount of sugar: there should be a ratio of 2¼ cups sugar to 2 cups juice.

Pour the juice back into the pan and bring to a boil. Add the sugar, cardamom seeds, and grapefruit zest and boil for 20–25 minutes, or until the gelling point has been reached—a candy thermometer should read 220°F. To perform the gel test, put ½ teaspoon of the jam on a chilled saucer, return it to the refrigerator or freezer for about 30 seconds or until cold, then prod the top. If a skin has formed, the jam is ready. If not, return to the heat to cook for a little longer and retest it.

Ladle the hot marmalade into the sterilized jars, filling to within ¼ inch from the top. Wipe rims with a clean, damp cloth. Seal jars with lids and screw bands. Label with the date and store in a cool, dark place for up to 6 months.

# Strawberry jam

2 lbs. slightly underripe strawberries, hulled and halved

3¾ cups sugar

freshly squeezed juice of 1 lemon

2 x half-pint preserving jars, sterilized (see page 4), with screw bands and new lids

**MAKES ABOUT 2 X HALF-PINT JARS**

Macerating strawberries in sugar overnight reduces the amount of cooking time, which in turn means that the strawberries aren't cooked to mush, but retain some of their texture. You have to really watch for the gelling point rather than relying on timing, as strawberries vary in water content and the more watery they are, the more cooking they will need.

Put the strawberries and sugar in a large nonmetal bowl. Cover and let sit overnight.

The next day, put 2 or 3 saucers in the refrigerator. Transfer the contents of the bowl to a wide saucepan and set over very low heat to dissolve any remaining sugar. Add the lemon juice and bring to a boil. Cook for 8–25 minutes, depending on the water content of the strawberries, or until the gelling point has been reached—a candy thermometer should read 220°F. To perform the gel test, put ½ teaspoon of the jam on a chilled saucer, return it to the refrigerator or freezer for about 30 seconds or until cold, then prod the top. If a skin has formed, the jam is ready. If not, return to the heat to cook for a little longer and retest it.

Ladle the hot jam into the sterilized jars, filling to within ¼ inch from the top. Wipe rims with a clean, damp cloth. Seal jars with lids and screw bands. Label with the date and store in a cool, dark place for up to 6 months.

# White chocolate praline spread

⅓ cup chopped almonds

6½ oz. white chocolate, chopped

1¼ cups heavy cream

2 x half-pint preserving jars

**MAKES ABOUT 2 X HALF-PINT JARS**

This is so naughty, but it is great for special occasions. I stole the idea from a Belgian café where they had this on the table for children. My feeling was that adults should share in this joy too. The chocolate mixture is just like making truffles, except when you spread it on hot toast, it melts into every pore.

Put the chopped almonds in a dry skillet over medium heat and let them heat up. Stir so they brown evenly, then remove from the heat.

Put the chocolate and cream in a heatproof bowl over a saucepan of gently simmering water. Do not let the base of the bowl touch the water and keep the heat low because white chocolate has a tendency to split. Let melt for 5 minutes. Remove from the heat and stir until smooth. Add the almonds and fold in.

Remove the bowl from on top of the pan and let cool completely. Transfer to the jars and refrigerate for up to 1 week. Bring to room temperature before eating.

*Strawberry jam (left)*

# index

## conversion chart

**Volume equivalents:**

| American | Metric | Imperial |
| --- | --- | --- |
| 6 tbsp butter | 85 g | 3 oz. |
| 7 tbsp butter | 100 g | 3½ oz. |
| 1 stick butter | 115 g | 4 oz. |
| 1 teaspoon | 5 ml | |
| 1 tablespoon | 15 ml | |
| ¼ cup | 60 ml | 2 fl.oz. |
| ⅓ cup | 75 ml | 2½ fl.oz. |
| ½ cup | 125 ml | 4 fl.oz. |
| ⅔ cup | 150 ml | 5 fl.oz. (¼ pint) |
| ¾ cup | 175 ml | 6 fl.oz. |
| 1 cup | 250 ml | 8 fl.oz. |

**Oven temperatures:**

| | | |
| --- | --- | --- |
| 170°C | (325°F) | Gas 3 |
| 180°C | (350°F) | Gas 4 |
| 190°C | (375°F) | Gas 5 |
| 200°C | (400°F) | Gas 6 |
| 220°C | (425°F) | Gas 8 |

**Weight equivalents:**

| Imperial | Metric |
| --- | --- |
| 1 oz. | 30 g |
| 2 oz. | 55 g |
| 3 oz. | 85 g |
| 3½ oz. | 100 g |
| 4 oz. | 115 g |
| 5 oz. | 140 g |
| 6 oz. | 175 g |
| 8 oz. (½ lb.) | 225 g |
| 9 oz. | 250 g |
| 10 oz. | 280 g |
| 11½ oz. | 325 g |
| 12 oz. | 350 g |
| 13 oz. | 375 g |
| 14 oz. | 400 g |
| 15 oz. | 425 g |
| 16 oz. (1 lb.) | 450 g |

**Measurements:**

| Inches | Cm |
| --- | --- |
| ¼ inch | 0.5 cm |
| ½ inch | 1 cm |
| ¾ inch | 1.5 cm |
| 1 inch | 2.5 cm |
| 2 inches | 5 cm |
| 3 inches | 7 cm |
| 4 inches | 10 cm |
| 5 inches | 12 cm |
| 6 inches | 15 cm |
| 7 inches | 18 cm |
| 8 inches | 20 cm |
| 9 inches | 23 cm |
| 10 inches | 25 cm |
| 11 inches | 28 cm |
| 12 inches | 30 cm |

## author's acknowledgments

A heartfelt thanks to the whole team at Ryland Peters & Small: to Céline for her eagle eye and Megan for her creative eye, as well as Alison for giving me this project in the first place. It has been a lifetime in the making, as breakfast has always been my favorite part of the day. Thanks to my wonderful, ever-reliable assistant Vorney for plowing through all the recipes with me in my kitchen and then again on the shoot. To Jonathan and Liz, what can I say? Your collaboration on this project has created the most beautiful breakfast and brunch book I have ever set eyes on. You are amazing! And lastly but by no means least, huge gushes of love to my husband and family who encourage and inspire me every day.